Unfiltered

The Long Winding Twisting Search for Self When You Were Never Missing in The First Place.

Kelly Anne Chester

To Kristy

A true Earth Angle

Thank you

Kelly xx

Copyright © 2022 by Kelly Anne Chester

Unfiltered

All rights reserved. No part of this publication may be reproduced, distributed or transmitted in any form or by any means,
including photocopying, recording, or other electronic or mechanical methods, without the prior written permission of the publisher, except in the case of brief quotations embodied in critical reviews and certain other non-commercial uses permitted by copyright law.

Although the author and publisher have made every effort to ensure that the information in this book was correct at press time, the author and publisher do not assume and hereby disclaim any liability to any party for any loss, damage, or disruption caused by errors or omissions, whether such errors or omissions result from negligence, accident, or any other cause.

Adherence to all applicable laws and regulations, including international, federal, state and local governing professional licensing, business practises, advertising, and all other aspects of doing business in the UK, US, Canada or any other jurisdiction is the sole responsibility of the
reader and consumer.

Neither the author nor the publisher assumes any responsibility or liability whatsoever on behalf of the consumer or reader of this material. Any perceived slight of any individual or organisation is purely unintentional.

The resources in this book are provided for informational purposes only and should not be used to replace the specialised training and professional judgement of a health care or mental health care professional.

Neither the author nor the publisher can be held responsible for the use of the information provided within this book. Please always consult a trained professional before making any decision regarding treatment of yourself or others.

For more information, contact www.thestretchzonemindgym.co.uk

ISBN: 9798420288320

Contents

As A Thank You For Buying My First Book	1
Dedication	3
Inspirational quote.	5
Forward by Mira Warszawski	7
Introduction	11
Chapter 1	25
Things are never what they seem.	
Chapter 2	33
My Yoga and Yin Yang Journey to recovery	
Chapter 3	47
My Journey into Reiki	
Chapter 4	59
Becoming a leader, The Wellbeing Network Years.	

Chapter 5	73
The travel and adventure years	
Chapter 6	83
When the comfort zone no longer feels comfortable, you need to get the hell out.	
Chapter 7	93
Network Marketing and Personal Development	
Chapter 8	107
Living with the long-term effects of stress and burnout.	
Chapter 9	115
Yoga Teacher Training	
Chapter 10	123
Visionary future aided by Visionary leaders	
Conclusion	143
Becoming unfiltered again	
Afterword by Jane Scanlan	149
Bonus Gift	153
Acknowledgments	161
About Kelly	163
Also By	165

As A Thank You For Buying My First Book

A free gift just for you.

Clear your Chakras and restore your body, mind, and spirit with no fancy equipment, just an open mind and no nasty comedowns.

You will be floating on air and feel like you are on holiday every day.

Spend a free month in the Beautiful Stretch Zone.

Three Videos for you to keep and use in your own time.

How to make the law of attraction work for you with ease and grace.

Balance your Chakras and increase your manifesting powers

Yin Yang Flow Class

Plus, a short, powerful healing Meditation

Come for your healing journey by visiting: www.thestretchzonemindgym.co.uk

You are taking the first step to becoming a more clear, calm, and confident you.

Dedication to my Grandad, who always believed in me and knew that I would one day make a difference in many people's lives. He inspired my story for The Trials and Tribulations of a Dyslexic Genius, a chapter in Wild Women Rising written by ten inspirational women who have changed their lives around.

The long twisting, winding roads to self-acceptance and the journey back to self-whilst being perfectly imperfect before being put into invisible boxes. Once out of the so-called boxes, she became truly visible.

Kellyisms by Kelly Chester

FORWARD BY MIRA WARSZAWSKI

I feel delighted and grateful for this amazing opportunity of writing a foreword to Kelly Chester's book: "Unfiltered."

People talk a lot about authenticity these days. Everyone wants to appear as an authentic person, leader, friend, business partner.

When others talk about it, Kelly Chester is being her authentic self in everything she does, and in fact, she has been living this way always which resonates with who she really is as a person. She remains true to herself and her core values of honesty, integrity, truthfulness, trust, respect, kindness, compassion for herself and others and non-judgemental attitude towards other human beings.

She knows what this feels like to be judged, having been through a lot of painful and uncomfortable experiences of being judged herself. She has been rejected so many times because of her hidden disability. She was labelled many names due to her dyslexia and dyspraxia. This had never stopped Kelly from following her passions and desires, aspiring to achieve more and live her life to the fullest on her own terms.

I have had this enormous pleasure to meet in person Kelly and her son Benjamin. She is an amazing mother and an unquestionable role model to her well mannered young son. They have a beautiful mum-son relationship, based on love, respect and understanding.

This is exactly what Kelly is aiming to imbue in her readers, shifting the paradigm in her stereotype breaking book "Unfiltered", teaching us how to speak openly about ourselves and how to break through labels placed upon us by society which quite often can be cruel due to lack of compassion and understanding.

Kelly inspires me with her thorough thinking of a heartfelt leader who has the courage within to speak up her truth without expecting external validation. She knows her worthiness and she understands her mission of helping others as a highly trained fitness instructor, intuitive healer, inspirational writer, yoga teacher with more than 20 years of experience. I have gained so much value from her online group "The Stretch Zone with Kelly." These weekly classes are an amazing way to care for our body and soul on a deeper level as Kelly takes her members on a journey of improving their health through exercises and soulful meditation.

Kelly is heartfelt and dedicated to everything she does, giving it all. This is why I believe she has an immense power of writing this incredible book from the perspective of being an expert in her field and truth preacher. She has a courageous heart full of loving kindness and this is what makes her stand out from the crowd. I wish her all the best in her private life and prosperity in her business modalities as an empowered business woman and influencer.

Introduction

My vision is to show that we are all the same, but different. We need to have that sense of connection and belonging. My dream is that one day we will no longer have labels or be seen as different due to the colour of our skin or our gender, age, or the way we dress or live our life. The diversity of the brain needs to be celebrated in all its glory. I want to help you see the world and the universe from a unique perspective. This book is not targeted at people with neurodiversity, and I hope you will see that you will benefit from this book if you are seen as neurotypical, which means learning in the so-called traditional way. We are not different, and we do not have a learning difficulty if we are put in the right environment. Let us learn and embrace each other's Gifts and give praise instead of making people feel not enough. We are all more than enough.

When we are born, we do not know what gender, colour, age, size, or what we are. It is only when we start to grow, we get influenced to live and be a certain way. We are born pure, and then we try to stay as we were when we were born and develop our natural skills and talents. If they are not perceived as the so-called norm, they get squashed down, and you grow up a different person. This does not have to be the case.

Unfiltered is about being dumbed down and being a watered-down version of yourself. Then becoming you again. This is about you choosing what you listen to and accept as your reality. You have a choice of how you fill your time and your mind. This is not a book about dictatorship leadership but one of true self-actualization. You have the tools already, and you need a gentle nudge to recalibrate and have a new perspective.

In this book, I can show you how you can be fully you and more confident, self-assured, and feeling full of self-belief. I have studied people from birth to the end of life. I started my career as a care assistant and worked my way up to an expert in my field. People want only one thing: to be truly seen for who they truly are with nothing missing. Your true authentic unapologetic, unfiltered self.

I have many methods in my tool kit from many decades of perfecting my Unique coaching gifts. You may not even notice that I am working on you as what I do has not been learned from a book. What I do is so gentle and subtle, learning from decades of practice, learning, and doing. I can help you find peace in an overwhelming world.

How many of you feel that there is more to life than just paying the bills? You have that nagging feeling that there must be more to life. We only know what we know, and it is only when we expand our comfort zones and start to question everything that we find out there is so much more. I am authoring this book for those who want to be more present, less stressed, calm, and totally in the now. We work increasingly to get more stuff that we do not need. Then we spend the weekends and spare time clearing up the stuff, and this makes us feel even more overwhelmed and stressed out.

This sounds extremely easy, but we have many distractions, and we spend hours scrolling mindlessly on social media and being a slave to the clock. Living for the weekends or home time. Often reaching for the fridge or the wine and then feeling like crap or bloated. Then your sleep pattern can be disrupted; then you start the next day on caffeine and lack of sleep, and the cycle begins again. The Stretch Zone Mind Gym was created from finding that calm space for myself; and it did not matter where I was in the world, as I could tap into the Stretch Zone.

I help busy people to live a calmer and more balanced life by showing them that they can live a simpler life. A simpler life with much less, a richer and fuller experience free of the trappings of a job you do not love, and finding time to do things that you want to do, like wanting to author a book, but never finding the time. I hear that lots of people want to write a book, and many have authored a book, but only about two percent get published.

I personally had no such desire to author a book, as living with Dyslexia made me believe that it would not be possible for me to author a book. Well, not in my own words. I then found a beautiful book strategist who helped me to write this in my own true voice. My why and vision became bigger than me.

I saw increased people in pain. With the work I have done on myself over the last few decades and the methods that I have learned and tried also have been tried on lots of my clients, they get results fast. For me, it is important to get my message out in all the different learning formats, as this was not the case for me. Even in higher education, this was not happening and I knew that I needed to speak up and make a difference. I have always been a leader and visionary.

I have a very curious and questioning mind.

My first word was why.

My ten-year-old son Benjamin is my inspiration for this book, just as my Grandad was my inspiration. This is about bringing in your younger self to your older self and giving you the best advice. Like myself, my son has neurodiversity, which is a spectrum disorder. We both needed labels to get access to essential support that we needed, but we will have no labels in the future. We will be truly holistic, see people as a whole, and celebrate life's tapestry of different brains. I have Dyslexia Dyspraxia and never thought I would be authoring a book. I want to show that at the end of the day, we all want the same thing: to be heard and seen. We need to celebrate our gifts and join to create something beautiful. What worked last century does not need to be carried forward. We can re-author the book that caters to our lovely individual's needs, wants, and desires. We cannot blame the past of the old systems; we need to make a stand and do something. Take some action and make a difference.

Who is this book for?

This is for anyone who wants to live a life of purpose and meaning.

Who has been put into a box and never wanted to be put into a box and want to get so far out of the box to be who they were before society and life tried to mould them into a box?

This is a real journey to self on a long, winding, far-reaching search for self and taking many detours and unexpected scenic routes along the way.

It is for anyone who wants to take that leap into the unknown and does not know how to.

You aspire to do much more with your life.

You feel like you are not living your best life.

You feel restless and want to live a life full of adventures and want to see life's full tapestry.

You feel like there is so much more to life than the material stuff.

You feel drawn to a higher way of living.

You are very down-to-earth and not necessarily drawn to the hippy-dippy world but want to embrace that inner hippy.

You like things simple and uncomplicated.

You have been told you are not fit for purpose or thick and will not amount to anything.

You have a real determination to prove that you are gifted and just need that helping hand to move you in the right direction after many wrong directions, or you had to go on those paths just to fit in.

I am not into hand-holding, but I will kick you up the glutes if I see your potential and help bring out your true purpose. I see in you what you may not see yourself and give you the belief and inspiration to get out there and shine brightly.

If you have read this far and not got bored, keep reading. I do get bored with a lot of books. If it does not grab me straight away, then I put it in a pile and never go back to it. A book and its words need to speak your language and enable you to feel that it is direct to you to which I am speaking. This is because I am.

These first few pages are the trailer to the movie which makes you want to know more or not.

I will not be offended if this happens to my book. I had this in a Facebook group. Somebody said it is very indulgent to author a book, and it will just end up in a dusty bookcase. She said you are just looking for validation. If I were doing that, I would not find the hardest route to write words down on a page. I would simply do a podcast and speak. I want to show that you can still write and get your voice across in a language that you speak. This is not about me, and if I inspire just one person from my words and experience, I will be an incredibly happy lady.

I want to get rid of the unconscious bias that if you have a hidden disability on the spectrum you don't still have beautiful gifts to share. I have had people speak slow to me when they find out I have dyslexia, and I need people to speak fast and not faff about. If you speak slowly, the screen saver goes on, and you have lost me. I use my humour a lot to cope in a world that did not embrace gifted individuals back in the 1970s, 1980s, and 1990s. We are slowly catching up, and one day we will not be seen as different and be accepted as our perfectly imperfect selves.

I hope that by sharing my truth, I will help others see that we do not grow out of dyslexia, dyspraxia, ADHD, or whatever label of diagnosis we may or may not have. We adapt, and sometimes we still need a bit of support after the age of eighteen. Many will not get a diagnosis until having children themselves, as those traits that you had will now be seen. Then that will often lead to many of us, who were told we were thick at school or not fit for purpose at work, to a diagnosis and finally feeling that we did well to get through life, but now know a reason for our difficulties.

I got into many scrapes and misadventures, which may have been prevented if I had the early support and guidance from an early age. I cannot turn back the clock, but I can help others by speaking up and talking to as many people as possible without the shame I had growing up.

I want to tell my story to inspire others and enable them to reach full actualization and find their sense of self and purpose.

If this resonates with you and you want to do the work to become the person you always wanted to be, then this is the book for you.

This is not about holding your hand and telling you everything will be ok. This is about you stretching your way out of your comfort zone and reaching self-actualization. It is not about settling; it is about stretching yourself to become who you are your true unapologetic, perfectly imperfect self.

It is never too late to rewrite the script.

Are you Ready?

I have re-written the script a vast number of times in my life. Sometimes I have stayed on the same chapter for far too long and kept re-doing the same chapter. Total and utter madness, but you do not know what you do not know until you find it out. I started to look out for others who were doing what I wanted to do for my upgraded life. I started to ask for advice and got as much information as I could. Now I am ready to share my knowledge and expertise. Being a self-made business person with no real clue what I was doing, in the beginning, was a challenge, but I had so much fun learning and did not realise that people were in the same situation as myself.

There are no fixed rules about how you live your best life. I just had this inner belief that I did not want to stay in a job working for someone else until I retired. I also knew that I did not want to get married and have kids at an incredibly youthful age. I wanted an adventure, and I well and truly had eventful adventures. Now I am fifty and ready to rewrite the script again.

My dream is to inspire others to go for what they want, despite not having all the skills to start with. I love connecting with people and teaching them how to do things they never thought possible.

Who am I?

This is a big question to ask yourself. We are all born in the same way, but we are not born with the same set of circumstances. My intro gives you a very brief insight into who I am today, and now I am ready to share the gifts that have worked for me and gave me that self-belief and confidence that I have today. I want you to think about that question as we do not get asked this. Many people go through life going through the motions. Give yourself the time to explore this. You can journal this, allow yourself to daydream, or just go for a walk. Have this in your mind when you are reading this book.

Becoming an entrepreneur

At an incredibly early age, I knew I felt different from other people. I spent hours just gazing into space and daydreaming. I was happiest outdoors, hanging upside-down and climbing trees. I was noticeably quiet at school and felt out of place most of the time. Even putting my hand up to ask to use the bathroom took a lot of courage. I was certainly not the strong, articulate, self-assured woman you see today. I struggled to keep up at school and was afraid to speak out because one of my first teachers was a true tyrant. She made us stand for what seemed like hours. I often fainted or had a nosebleed when the pressure got to be too much, and I spent a lot of time outside the classroom. I could not keep up with the writing on the chalkboard. They erased it before I had time to catch up. That class was a living hell.

Homelife was a more bohemian way of living and could not be more different than school. My mum was a single mum, which was unusual in the 1970s. I spent a lot of time with my grandparents whilst my mum was at work part-time, and I loved spending time with my Nanna and Grandad.

Nanna had rheumatoid arthritis and struggled to do physical activities and daily chores. I helped her with various activities of daily living. Grandad was the one who inspired me, though. He knew I struggled with schooling and helped me build up my confidence. I struggled with rules and school, but what Grandad taught inspired me. He told me, "I am going to teach you how to survive. But what you are about to learn is not something they can teach you at school." He showed me that the way you look after others is incredibly special and worth more than any exam result. He taught me that the way that you make people feel is more important than what you accomplish.

This encouragement became my first insight into becoming an entrepreneur and the businessperson I am today. I earned money by doing small errands like cleaning cars, going to the shops, and running jumble sales outside the house. My grandad wrote a sign that said, "Jumble Sail." This sign drew people who came up and said, "You spelt that wrong," but they stayed to chat and ended up buying something. Grandad was a very clever man and beyond his time. I still use his method whatever I am selling to this day, and it does work. People are quick to judge and will always point out a mistake. But often we strike up a conversation and they end up becoming my friend or taking one of my services.

In school, I was called "thick" and told I would not amount to anything. Teachers were not sure what to do with me. I left school at 16 with incredibly low grades but I was so glad to leave school as early as possible. I have blanked out most of my school days. I tried extremely hard every day and still got low grades. Others were hardly at school and got better grades than me. I was so glad to get away from academics and begin working. I was put on a YTS care assistant training course. My years looking after

Nanna gave me the skills to do the more practical kind of work that is still seen as low-skilled to this day.

Care work was hard, but I loved it. I also got into the rave scene, which was a welcome break from reality. I partied hard and often went to work on little sleep. At 18, I moved to London and soon got a job in care work.

I had my first long-term, committed relationship from the age of 21 to 27. His university mates looked down on me because I was not at university like them, but he stood up for me and kept pushing me. I went on to try and pass my entrance exam to be a nurse. I tried several times but could not pass the test. This setback did not stop me. I went to college to learn to use the computer and touch type. This skill was amazing as my brain works amazingly fast, and for the first time in my life, I was able to write my thoughts down before I forgot what I wanted to write. Yet, I was not word-perfect and still struggled with grammar and spelling.

At my job, I continued to develop skills to build my way up the ranks and became a senior care assistant in charge of the domestic staff and administering the patients' drugs. Ironically, I was not good enough to pass the entrance exam to become a nurse, but was put in charge of the drug trolley. I was incredibly good at my job and passed all my NVQ courses at level 111 and became an NVQ assessor. As I assessed my students, others asked me, "Are you not going to write the answers all down?" as I assessed my students. I replied, "No need as I have their responses all stored in a television set in my head." That skill was easy for me though I did not understand why.

I still had a hunger for learning and decided I wanted to go to university. I earned a place at the Open University, working towards my diploma in Health and Social Welfare. The real turning point in my studies occurred when I got pulled into the office. The professor told me my written work did not match my oral comprehension. She scheduled me for a dyslexia test. I had a tutor sent to my house for the two-hour assessment, and at the age of 23, it was finally confirmed that I had dyslexia. The university assigned me my tutor and extra time for my exams. I was also sent all my books on audio cassettes, which were created by the RNIB. I listened to them on a Walkman whilst riding on the train, doing chores, and any spare moment I had. I still learn better by listening to this day, but now I find information on podcasts, TED Talks, and YouTube.

I love reading and read an average of five books a month, mainly books on personal development and spirituality. Reading has never been a problem for me. Only other people's perception of someone with dyslexia. I read extremely fast and process fast. It is in the saying back what I have just read in a way that makes sense to others. It makes perfect sense to me but may seem backwards to others. I spent my childhood reading and during my university years, it was tough how to pick out the main parts and do a summary of the books I have read. I read newspapers like this. Cut out all the irrelevant bits and get the main body of the story. If something interests me then I will read the whole lot.

I went to incredibly special training with other students who had dyslexia, and each of our tutors came. We were all asked to recall what was in our living room. Those with dyslexia could remember the details with ease and grace, but the tutors struggled to do this.

This is where I came into my own and want to share my incredibly special unique journey with you and share my passion for learning and inspiring others to tap into their unique gifts with ease and grace. This is where I came into my own when I finally realised why I could so easily evaluate student responses on their NVQ assessments. I had minute attention to detail to cross-reference all eight units very easily in my brain's skill. I also drew out their best qualities and got them to pass.

It took me five years to complete my diploma. Most finished in two years, but I worked full-time while taking classes. It also took me longer to learn how to fit into the academic world. It was like learning a new language. My favourite book and film were Educating Rita. Working-class women going to University - I wanted that. Leaving school at 16, University was not an option for me until years later.

One of my life's proudest moments was when I passed and completed my diploma. It was even more special as I did think I was capable of much more. I always tried so hard at school but could not understand why despite always trying so hard I could not pass my exams. Having the right tests and the right strategies to help with my unique learning style was a real notable change for me.

Fast forward to age 27, I came out of my long-term relationship and had to restart my life again. I had my first real bout of stress and burn-out, which stopped me in my tracks. Something was missing in my life. I achieved a lot in my life, but felt empty and wanted more from my life. I was feeling, "is this it?"

Let me start with a story that is funny now, but at the time was a very dark night of the soul period of my life. It is in those dark periods that you truly grow. We do not grow in our comfort zones. You will be amazed at the gifts once you have pushed through your comfort zone.

Chapter 1

Things are never what they seem.

From the outside, I looked like I had it all - a relationship, well-paid job, two-income salary home, and holidays. It was not all that it seemed. I felt very trapped as my ex-fiancé was suffering from bipolar; it was called manic depression back in the 1990s and had a real stigma. He was descending further and further into the darkness, and I felt increasingly trapped.

I was trying to do as much as I could at work to distract myself from my personal life. I saw an advert to do a parachute jump for charity, so I decided to raise some money for the day centre where I worked. I fully immersed myself in this and got a team together. We went down for the training session, and reality was starting to kick in. I was jumping out of a plane thousands of feet in the air. The training sessions were fun, and the excitement was growing.

Over the next week, we heard that somebody had died doing a parachute jump at HeadCorn where we were doing our parachute. I had this in the back of my head and was bricking myself. I was exceptionally good at masking and just got on with things. The day of the parachute jump arrived and I got my kit on and went up in the plane. I was given clear instructions on which way to go. I was not doing this as a tandem; I was totally doing this on my own with no expert strapped to me. I was in control of pulling the parachute out myself. Always check your own parachute.

This will become clear very soon. It was time to fly, one elephant, two elephants, three elephants, and go. It was so noisy up in the air, and I felt free as a bird. I heard the radio going, and it was saying, go this way. I forgot to consider that my direction of left and right was not great on land, never mind thousands of feet in the air. I just wanted to fly and be free. Free of the relationship, free of the obligations, and needed to escape.

I pulled the parachute and began to glide through the air going totally in the wrong direction. Not for me though, this felt right, and I was admiring the view.

Or was I? I knew it was not the end of my life but knew I wanted out from my current life.

Madness or Magnificence

Madness or magnificence - it is an exceptionally fine line. It was mesmerising and the closest I could get to heaven whilst still alive and free. I saw the ground coming closer and closer and almost landed on a sheep. I packed up my parachute and looked around. I saw a pub across the field. I popped in and said, "I do not have any money on me as I have just done a parachute"; nobody offered me a pint—what a shame. I had a lady say "you were lucky you did not land in the lion's den over there." She said, "do not worry as he has no teeth. He would have just mauled you to death." I was not really taking it in as I was a tad shell-shocked.

This same kind lady drove me back to HeadCorn. I got such a telling off from the crew and got told I was banned for life and that I could not be trusted to do another one due to not following orders.

I felt a bit battered and bruised for a bit. It was more the sheer velocity and gee force of flying out the plane. I love the tune "Free Falling" by Tom Petty. I was taking a leap of faith and jumping into the unknown. Not long after that, my relationship ended, and I was free.

Recently, I went on holiday and did high ropes. They asked me if I had done any high ropes before. I said I had jumped out of a plane and said I did it alone. They said, do you not have to do 25 jumps before doing that? I said I never, and this was back in the 1990s. It was then it truly dawned on me that I had done it. Pack your own parachute; you oversee your destiny. Be brave and take that leap; well, maybe not as extreme as me, but you get my point.

Back to age 27, I came out of my relationship and had to restart my life again. I had my first real bout of stress and burnout, which stopped me in my tracks. I decided to clean up my life, stopped the party lifestyle, and got into yoga and spirituality. Something was missing in my life. I had achieved what many had said would be impossible for me. Not because I was dyslexic, but because I was a care assistant; we were still classed as the lowest of the low. This is so not true, and we were the real heart of the caring profession—highly skilled and exceptionally long hours with all the studying in our own time.

I got serious about my yoga and enjoyed boxing training: big contrast but life's natural yin and yang. I had a lot of frustration and anger at me at times due to how hard it was for me to pass exams. I got very frustrated with my work in care eventually and wanted to get more into my passion for teaching exercise. Burnout and stress are creepers. You do not realise you are burning out until you get sick, or you get aches and pains, and all the joy is being sucked from you.

I loved my job in social care but with cuts and austerity, the workload just got heavier and heavier. My back was bad with all the heavy manual labour, minimal breaks, and not enough time to eat properly. Plus, the clients were also getting heavier. Not due to any health issues but due to not being able to move around as much and the ageing process. It is hard enough to stay in shape as a fully functioning, able-bodied person. It is a double whammy if you add health and mobility problems to the mix.

Many care workers or service providers in the health service are very prone to burnout due to their caring nature and wanting to help others. Often people are pleasers and go above and beyond to help others. The more cuts, the more you try to keep people alive and well. It made me very resourceful and imaginative and still run interesting and fun services despite the tiny budgets we were given.

So I started going to a class called Yin Yang, and my teacher helped me get my back stronger, and I was able to function much better. I went to Iyengar yoga to fix my mind and go to restorative yoga every Saturday for about three hours. It was a real oasis of calm in the middle of a remarkably busy South London borough. I was not able to do the hard classes due to a car accident; this took me two years to recover.

My personal life was in a mess. I had come out of a long-term relationship and did not have much spare cash. London is a wonderful place but expensive. So other than the gym membership, I did not have much leftover for much else. The health club was my sanctuary and was always the one thing that kept me going. Then my back went, and I was struggling with the heavy work and needed to be put on light duties. After work, I was still going to the gym to use the sauna and steam to help my recovery. I had a few whisperings behind my back that I cannot be that bad if I was still going to the gym.

There was a lot of slagging off in the so-called caring profession. It is very much a high-pressure environment. You never got much praise and only really got pulled into the office when you have made a mistake.

It was all about keeping you in fear of your job and telling you that you are not fit for purpose if you do not fulfil your role, even though we often worked in very unsafe ways. Every member of the team was suffering from muscular-skeletal issues and stress-related issues.

I stayed in that job a lot longer than I should have, and I always remember something that a guy called Alan Shearer said - no, not the footballer but a true legend of social care. He met me when I was young and enthusiastic and about 21 or 22. He said never let them knock that enthusiasm out of you. If that ever happens then, it is time to leave.

I knew it was time to leave when I was part of a team-building day. I used to love team-building days. A question was asked what three things you love about your job. I sat with a colleague and put on holiday, home time, and payday. They saw what I had written and said, you cannot put that. I said, but this is the truth. I never said it aloud and made some shit up just to fit in with the joke of the team building day.

After austerity and cuts, there was no longer a team - just survival. It was at that point that I knew I needed to get out. I had been whining about the job for years but felt trapped by the mortgage, debts, and not knowing which direction to go in. I kept the faith and knew that all the studying and the love of learning would pay off one day. I just needed to get out before this job killed me or made me extremely sick. Many of my colleagues and friends were not so lucky and were sent on the capability route and no longer fit for purpose.

I want people to get out of these jobs and toxic ways of living before it destroys them. For me, I am still living with the effects of those times living with a chronic illness and a bad back. With careful management and self-care, I barely notice anymore. I teach all the self-care techniques that I have tried and tested myself in my classes.

The job itself was one I loved, and the people I worked with were like family. We worked in one of the better places with fantastic equipment and services. It was the cuts and austerity that broke us. Are things any better 20 years on? This is a question you need to ask yourself.

Personally, I believe it is much worse now. We are just coming to the end of a global pandemic and cannot credit the NHS and the social care workers enough. They are going to be coming out of this with trauma and PTSD. They will have seen such horrors daily, so hopefully, systems will be put into place to help those who have looked after our loved ones, putting themselves and their family members at risk and may be suffering from long Covid. Many will never recover.

Profit before people will never work long term, and we need to bring the community back together. Without the army of carers, local volunteers, mothers looking after both children and ageing relatives we have a breakdown in social care and the long-neglected system. We stopped people from getting too sick due to loneliness and taking the strain away from the NHS. Taking money from the social care budget was a big mistake. I got told to shut up about this a lot. I looked at the longer-term vision and not short-term profit to pay the suits.

I am still friends with the people I worked with within social care, and we have lots of very fond memories. It takes a special person to serve others at their most vulnerable. We are not "just" care assistants. We were the glue bridge between the families and the doctors and consultants. So, stop treating carers as the lowest of the low. Give them the recognition and the pay rise that they truly deserve.

I went to see some of my old work friends, and they mentioned people having to sell homes to get the care paid for if they needed care. People selling their homes is not a new thing; this was happening when I started 34 years ago. It is a very unfair system and needs to be looked at from a deeper perspective. Ask those who have seen it from the front line. I went to university and studied the damaging effects of increasing cars and out of town supermarkets. I authored an essay on the effects of losing the high street and the obesity crisis. I wrote this 20 years ago.

The high street was the glue of the community. Fresh local produce and people walk to the shops without using the car. I am Generation X, and we do not get mentioned very much. It is mainly Baby Boomers and Millennials. We are now stepping up and leading the way to protect the older generation and guide the younger generation through life's lessons. We were like the lost generation. We got told we could have it all but ended up feeling inadequate trying to be perfect.

I have only really seen this since becoming a mother. There was less choice for my mother's generation but a more clear path. We may be living longer, but we need to live longer in good health. Not years of illness and disease. Prevention is always better than cure. So, if they had listened to the hidden army years ago, we could be living a vastly different life. Hindsight is wonderful, and we cannot dwell on these things. I will continue to keep making a difference. I may no longer be in social care, and I still put back into the community, just in a different capacity.

Chapter 2

My Yoga and Yin Yang Journey to Recovery

I wanted to keep yoga special for me, so I did not train as a Vinyasa yoga teacher until 2018. I have been living as a yogi long before it became trendy. I have never been hippy-dippy, though, not that I have nothing against this. I just wore what I wanted, and if it was practical, I was happy. There is nothing worse than leggings falling and flashing tomorrow's washing. I practised yoga to find peace of mind and calm. After practising yoga, I loved how I felt and enjoyed being part of the yoga community.

My years working in social care helped me find my love of working within the community. I love getting people to connect on and offline. Being a single mum got me out and about, and I met lots of lovely people in the local area.

This enabled me to see that many people in my situation wanted to get fitter or wanted to learn and develop their skills. Many had the same blocks as me, which was not getting out in the evenings, low income, or careers. Not everyone can dedicate an hour of their time to go to a class, and yoga is about fitting into the knucks and crannies of the day or night. Even at 3 a.m. if this suits you. I started my yoga practice at 12 years old in my bedroom. I didn't even have a yoga mat: just me and a book. Yoga is an internal practice and not one that is about looking good. Yoga is about community and connection.

Many decades later, this was my brainchild to build an online platform. A few months before a global pandemic, I had the idea for my online classes to help those who want to go to yoga or exercise classes. I wanted to keep it affordable and accessible for those on low incomes. My passion is to enable as many people to access my knowledge as possible. I would be teaching in my small corner of the world, thinking about how I could get more people to look after themselves. Whilst in social care, there was only so much I could do. Care work was no longer about caring but money savings and cuts; it was not going into the right places.

The suits took over, and they had no clue how people and caring for others truly worked. No disrespect to the suits as they were faceless people to me. We never saw them and they did not know what we did. The heart and soul of the community were at the grassroots. I now feel like this time is coming back. Money and greed are not how the circle of life works. I remember watching many of my clients from being young and vibrant to being broken down by the system. We live in a broken society, and it took a global pandemic for people to realise the actual value. Being a care assistant was a true blessing as I got to see people without the mask on, no trappings of material positions and just a room with a few memories and maybe a few visitors.

A few of the clients did not get visitors until it was too late, and then the fights may start if the person had any money left after paying for extortionate care costs. The food was often of extremely inadequate quality, and one would have been better going on a cruise all year round and hiring a carer or two to take care of them. They would have entertainment, clean towels, and room service. Plus, a chance to see the world. Not just seen as a burden to society. We need to know the value in our forgotten army of carers and those with disabilities and hidden gifts.

I learned so much from my beautiful clients. One was a doctor, and he had just qualified. The day he qualified, he got run over outside the hospital and was very severely damaged and could never work again. He was a real pain in the proverbial backside but a loveable pain. Imagine being in your prime with a gifted brain and then having a body that no longer functions, and you are dependent on others to wipe your backside and deal with all your care needs. Therefore, I am passionate about keeping people healthy and well to live a full and independent life and fully sharp within the mind. Many ended up with a physical disability because they became sick in the mind with anxiety, stress, depression, trauma, PTSD, and not fitting into a so-called box. My days were spent trying to fit people into boxes as people were not seen as a whole person.

My passion for yoga, boxing, and healthy living worked its way to my clients, and I became one of the main staff members to incorporate new classes and initiatives within the daycare centre where I worked for 15 years. Boxolates was born from this place. I created the seated yoga and added the boxing to enable my clients to get rid of the pent-up frustration and energy. Can you imagine being in your 20s and at this stage of life, with a disability and sex had been very much taboo?

Until I worked at the day centre, I worked mainly with the older generation. They were still very sexual, and many were in their 90s. I had to stop a few randy clients in my time. I needed to make sure that one guy did not get into ladies' rooms as he was a naughty man, and some of the ladies were still virgins or had not even been seen naked by anybody. Not even their husbands.

Working with young men and women was different. They needed to be able to express themselves. We were very much ahead of the game and a very forward-thinking team who wanted the best for our clients. No subject was taboo. Imagine being a young adult and having a care system telling you how to live every aspect of your life. Thank goodness we have people like myself to lead the way. London was amazingly diverse, and I loved learning about diverse cultures, different food choices, and the music.

How did I get into boxing training? That came about by accident. I was fighting with my current boyfriend and punched him. It was a lot harder than anticipated, and he said you need to take up boxing or something. I do not know where that anger came from, but I knew I needed to channel it. Many people, especially young men with dyslexia, often end up in prison. Little was known about neurodiversity back in the 1970s, 1980s, and early 1990s.

I worked in Herne Hill and saw a poster daily about a Boxercise class above a pub. I decided to pop in after work to look. It was a traditional boxing gym with just the basics - a ring and skipping ropes with a few simple machines and weights. Clinton McKenzie, who was three times World Champion back in the 1990s, ran it. I signed up for my first class, and it was hard. I could barely walk for three days, but I was hooked.

Duke McKenzie was also part of the gym, and when he was close to retirement, he started to help at the gym. I was sparring with him, and he said, you are one of the fastest at sparring that I have ever met. Duke was also a three times Welterweight World Champion boxer. One of the highlights of my life was sitting in the changing room, putting on my bandages, and sitting in between two World Champion boxers. I looked at either side and thought to myself, this does not happen every day.

How did Boxolates start? I continued to hurt after boxing training, so I started to add more yoga stretches into my workout. For example, during the skipping, I would skip for three minutes and stretch during the one-minute rest. This minimised the amount of time that I needed to rest. Boxing training did help me emotionally and mentally, and the guys I met at boxing were the calmest and nicest people you could meet. Few women or girls were doing this back in the 1990s. I feel very privileged that I was able to give it a go and be able to teach this method to this day still. I am not up to twelve rounds of three minutes of skipping but still fit.

Now aged 50, I am back to teaching Boxolates. I had some marketing content done for me in lockdown and noticed that it spelt Boxilates. I messaged the lady to say it was spelt wrong. I did not get a response back, so continue to use my marketing. I then started to work at a new place with the same spelling. I was told that it was the way it was spelt and was shown that there is a whole program about Boxilates. I never knew this as I created Boxolates, and I do not look at what others do. I am a creator and too busy creating my own systems. I started this method because I was trying to minimise how much I was hurting after training. It was only later that I realised how many more people with dyspraxia and hypermobility were more prone to joint pain and injuries. I had developed a system without realising it, which has benefited hundreds if not thousands of my clients.

Kinesthetic Learning in all that I do. Utilising the senses and feelization.

I use food, healing, and music in all that I do. Even writing this now, I have the candles and incense burning. The music is playing, and the beautiful essential oil baths are all part of the process of writing. This practice ended up filtering into the day centre. The morning session was "Exercise," and the afternoon session was "Relaxation," where I would light candles and oils and get the clients onto bean bags. Being in a chair was hard on joints all day, so this was true bliss. I started by playing Louisa Hay and a few tapes with positive visualisations and mantras. My clients loved it, and as I got more confident, I started to make my own up. A few sessions were far out, and one client asked me what medication I was on. I have this gifted brain that takes me on many adventures in my mind.

My clients had difficulty travelling to places, but I would take them on mind adventures. I love mind adventures and travel to beautiful destinations when I find something tedious. Luckily, I fill my days with doing mostly what I enjoy, so I need to book in a time now to have mind adventures, and this is where my daily reiki sessions come in, which is in the next chapter.

This group started to grow extremely popular, and students and staff would join in if they had a break. I was ahead of my time. It was a fabulous way to shut down the busy brain for a while and recharge the batteries ready for the afternoon transport sessions and the journey home. Mindfulness was not a thing back in the 1990s, and early 2000s. I felt thrilled that I had the creativity to create my classes for my clients.

You may be thinking about what this has to do with yoga. This has everything to do with yoga. Yoga is for everybody and not about looking pretty on a lilypad chanting "om." Although that does look aesthetically pleasing to the Instagram culture. We were not too bothered in the 1990s, and the Nokia mobile phone had come out then. No fancy camera phones that are glued to us now 24/7. The day I got a smartphone was the day I became a slave to my phone and an addict, just like many others.

The Yoga Institute in south London was a haven away from the outside world. No phones, no egos, total bliss, and a bit of torture at times for a few hours. Real old-school yoga. With a look of an old run-down building from the outside, inside was a vast oasis of calm and some knowledge from the teachers directly from the source; from Mr. Iyengar himself, channelling his energy down from his masters and directly to my teachers.

Being a Yogi is not an exercise system; it is a way of life and responsibility. It is a genuine compliment to be chosen as a teacher. Back then, I loved the idea of being a teacher, but I loved learning and observing the teachers learning to teach yoga. I had far too much ego, and my party girl spirit was still in full force.

I was not up to a full-on yoga class though due to my back. I injured my back at the age of 17 as a care assistant. There were no hoists back then, and we would manually lift people. I was still not fully grown and not fully strong. I was in the deep end and often worked alone. My back continued to deteriorate over the years. My teacher advised me to come along to Restorative Yoga on a Saturday. It was not full-on yoga but more my style, but it was one of the hardest things I have ever done. It was meant to be a two-hour class, but it often lasted for three hours.

The teachers and helpers helped us all to get into various positions using bolsters, bricks, straps, chairs, and blankets. I was often in a lot of pain, but I was taken care of by these beautiful yogis who were learning to be teachers for these few hours. I also observed what they were doing and took in all the teaching points. I was not ready to be a yoga teacher and enjoyed being a pupil. The training was very disciplined for both students and teachers. I started to get more and more into the yogi way. I cut drastically down on meat, went plant-based, and hardly drank. I stopped smoking and was living an exceptionally clean life.

My weekends started to be more about clean living and coffee shops, markets and becoming more bohemian. I had my flat, I was living alone, and I was doing as I genuinely wanted for the first time. I had always lived with people until I owned my place.

I was also a member of a gym and would be doing weights and cardio. I was strong and not the typical yoga teacher body despite all of this. I would often get "how come with all your exercise and healthy food you are not skinnier?" I was very slim moving to London but built myself up after hurting my back. I was doing a big manual job. I was much slimmer when doing the boxing training, but it no longer served me as my back was not getting any better, and yoga was helping me more.

Yin Yang and Meeting Harold Coggins

At the gym, I met a guy called Harold. He was teaching kids kung fu. I went into the studio to get a yoga mat. He shouted at me to say it was a private class and not to walk into the studio. I was a bit hot-headed back then and came out and said, "who is that?" I was not sure about him. I continued to watch the class with curiosity and got invited in. Yes, it was a kid's class but I decided to give it a go. My coordination was not the best, but the kids were not bothered. They just said, "OK, go again." I still have that patience, and taking 200 takes to get my yoga video was no mean feat. I just kept going until it was done. I get that a lot. Many tell me I would have given up long before. I just think, well, what else I would be doing. May as well keep trying until I perfect it. I think this stems from being an only child. I had no one to compare myself to and nobody to shut me down. The tenacious nature has always been there.

I joined the adult class one day, and we had to line up. I got asked if I had done this before. I said "no." A guy, twice the size of me, was my partner. I did a move, and he went to the floor. He looked at me and said, "are you sure you have not done this before?" "Nope, but I learned how to fight at school." It was one thing I did learn at school. How to survive. Fighting was a daily occurrence on the school field. I learned to fight so that I did not have to.

I started to attend Harold's Yin Yang class on a Sunday morning. So, it was Saturdays at the Yoga Studio and Sundays at the Health Club and Spa. I had no time for the party life anymore and was addicted to a new high. Feeling fit and healthy. Mentally I felt good, and I was physically getting strong.

Then something devastating happened. I was driving home and just around the corner from my workplace as I was at the traffic lights in stationary traffic, I got shunted from the back. I was involved in a car accident that would truly mess up my back even more. I left my car and went straight to A and E at Kings College Hospital. They did not pick up much, but the following few days, I had full-on whiplash. All my right sides were shattered. I had gone from getting my legs to my ears standing up to barely being able to lift my legs from the floor more than a few inches.

The next few days were a blur, and I could not work for a while. I booked in to see an osteopath privately and got half of it paid for out of a privacy policy that I took out. I waited a long time to get a payout for my injuries, and it was only a couple of grand.

Why is it you get so little when you do damage to your body but get a bigger payout for processions? I decided to book a holiday out of the money. I booked a sailing holiday to the Caribbean in Grenada. I was so excited, and then another devastating thing happened. They had a hurricane in Grenada, and the whole island was affected. I was at Salability at the time when the news hit, and the crew thought I might be terribly angry about losing my holiday.

I was not angry, just so upset for the beautiful people on the island who had just lost their homes. I got offered another holiday, so all was good. I ended up in Turkey on a more relaxing holiday, which was much more suitable for me to recover. I often think back to my sailing days when life went a bit wrong, and you felt like you wanted to get off the treadmill. The clearing forest fire removes the dead wood ready to clear and bring in the new growth. Grenada recovered, and so did my car accident injuries. They only came up to let me know I need to take better care of myself.

Having a chronic back condition is the very reason that I can help many others who suffer from backache and other muscular conditions. There are always blessings in the lessons. You think what the fuck is happening at the time, but you do get through it. It may take a while - even a few years and even decades. Some people only discover these breakthroughs and aha moments on their deathbed. "The Top Five Regrets of the Dying" by Bronnie Ware is an amazing book. Nobody ever said I wish I spent more time at the office.

Universal laws and the Law of Attraction

Working in service and serving people for most of my life has given me such precious gifts and insights. I have seen how people are at the end of life, and it is absolutely beautiful hearing many of the stories. Some are honestly sad, and all that is left is a small room and just a few memories. Make as many memories as you can before they begin to fade. Accidents are never an accident; these come into your life to make you stop and take a stop and be present. So, stop worrying so much about the past. You cannot change it, just what you have learned, and you cannot control what happens in your future.

Anxiety is related to catastrophizing and not trying new things because you think things might happen and never do. Catastrophizing in our minds what might happen. Things very much never happen as you expect them to, and quite often, it is even more magical than you could ever imagine.

If you are moving too fast and not getting anywhere, then the universe will make you do a detour so that you slow down and take time out. If we are busy rushing around and filling our time with no time to reflect, then we must be available to rest. If you do not listen and run the engine into the ground, you must be available for illness. When I get ill now, I call on my beautiful friends, ask for reiki, heal, and start to look at what is not serving me. It is mainly eating too much of the wrong things.

Life is about balance and the polarities of life - the yin and yang and the masculine and the feminine. We need this to work with the Law of Attraction. The universe does not hear the word not or no. Just the same as when I did my exams, I do not pick up double negatives in sentences. It needs clear instructions. Not poshed up overcomplicated sentences.

Setting a clear goal and intention is key to getting what you want and desire. If you focus on lack, you will get more lack and when you raise your vibration and in abundance, then the universe is sending everything you desire fast. The Law of Attraction loves speed. Once you put your order in, do not interfere with it, as this is like ordering a meal and keep sending it back. You need that clear intention, and then you start to become that person who is ready to receive.

It takes work, and it is not about just sitting back waiting for things to fall on your lap. Authoring this book has been all about using the Law of Attraction. I had no idea where the money would come from or who would be the people who would help me to make this happen. I had decided it would happen, and it is. I was confident that Sandra would be the midwife for my book, which was non-negotiable.

Chapter 3

My Journey into Reiki

Just before my 30th Birthday, I started to question everything; I have always had a very curious nature and had many years of people telling me that I think too much in my head. I thought to myself, where else would I be thinking? What a strange thing to say. You only really know from your reality, and you do not know what you do not know until you are catapulted into a world of the unknown. You need to imagine, and then reality follows according to your reality. No two people's perception is ever the same. This is what makes life wonderful and celebrates our perfectly imperfect imperfections and quirks.

Now, this is what makes us unique, but this can be exceedingly difficult when you have had to comply with the so-called norm or the new normal, what is normal. I have had to filter my mind to fit into what I see as a very bland world. My world is a giant, massive kaleidoscope of colours in my brain, and I see the world in high definition.

So, the journey began into the spiritual world. I went to a show with my best mate, and we saw a Reiki stall advertising a Reiki training retreat. We both decided to book it. Things started to go wrong, and the event fell through, and we struggled to get our deposit back. Eventually, we got it back—a big blessing in disguise. I did not think about Reiki again for a few months as my dad had cancer, and it was a tough time.

To take my mind off things, I went to a local Mind Body Spirit Fair in Catford in south London, which was down my street. I was drawn to a table with a purple cloth and decided to have a reading. She said you are about to embark on an amazing spiritual journey and use your gifts. She also went very deep and was spot on with lots of deep stuff that nobody would have known. She gave me a cassette to keep for me to check on later. I still have this cassette and it talks about my nanna and grandad looking out for me.

I walked away in a daze and went to a Reiki stall, and a lovely guy was standing there and shook my hand. I felt this amazing energy surge through me. I thought, wow. It was not sexual chemistry but a real connection. We got talking, and I signed up for his Reiki course on the other side of London. This time all the organising and getting to the course went swimmingly. Everything felt right and inflow. It was over four evenings over two months. I signed up for Reiki 1 and Reiki 11 at the same time, not knowing what I had let myself in for. I was new to all this, so I was not sure what would happen.

By the time my course had started, I had lost my dad to cancer, so all was raw. I arrived at Gary's house and met three other people who were doing the course with me. It was a very enjoyable evening, and I had the very first Reiki Attunement; there are four with Reiki 1. It was a long time ago, so I cannot remember if I had the four in one go or over four weeks. I know I floated home and got on with the 21-day spiritual path of keeping a journal and doing self-treatments daily. I was not sure where my head was for a while but loved doing the daily self-treatment for an hour a day. I still practice this every day 20 years down the line. Just three short years earlier, I struggled to stay still, but because of Restorative Yoga, I got exceptionally good at relaxing. I have now got down to fine art. Gary even said I was like a corpse. Well, that is the non-Sanskrit name for Savasana.

Reiki 1 is all about loving yourself and treating yourself first. It is also about practising with friends, family, animals, and even plants and food. I watched Gary turn cheap wine into nice-tasting wine. Not a skill I was expecting in reiki. I have learned many gifts since but will save that for a bit later. I was not ready for those until two decades later.

The journey to Gary's house was weird. It took me a long time to get there the first time and then the next time I got there earlier and earlier. Gary could see I was struggling on one visit and did a Reiki session on me before the others arrived. I was still very raw from grief, but did not know how to deal with it. He said Reiki gives you what you need and not what you want. It is not all love and light and pretty sparkles. It brings up your raw emotions from a very deep level. I spent my time journaling and kept doing the Reiki daily and writing down all of my thoughts and feelings. I still write in my journal to this day, and it is very unfiltered.

What was apparent was the world seemed brighter, and I started to feel a few shifts. A book that I had forgotten I had ordered arrived, and this was a book on Chakras. I use the Chakras in lots of my meditations, and it feels fantastic. I got so hungry for learning and started to read everything I could on crystals, chakras, and personal development books. I had tapped into them a few years before, and I was absorbing them this time. My first book was "The Road Less Travelled and Beyond" by M. Scott Peck. I have always had a deep fascination with psychology and what makes people tick.

My take on that book was there are two types of people in the world, those who think the world owes them and those who believe that they are the givers of the world. The empaths are there to serve others and be humble with them. I now see that as the energy drainers and the energy givers.

The book that changed my life was Louise Hay's "You Can Heal Your Life." She was ahead of her time, and I still listen to her regularly. I based a lot of my meditations on Louise Hay. I do not need a script as I know them all word for word. They say it takes 10,000 hours to become an expert in anything. I am an expert and a pioneer in helping others to relax truly.

After practising Reiki 1 for a month, it was time for Reiki 11. Wow, I did not expect to feel Reiki 11 so strongly, but I was flying for days. I also cried a lot. I am not a crier, and this was a shock, but I had to go with it. I have seen people cry in yoga and wonder why they are crying from just doing yoga. I did not understand yoga even though I had practised it from the age of 12. I still had to go to work, which felt better than any self-medication that I had ever tried in the past. I was well and truly hooked.

I had tried a lot of self-medicating during my raving years, and I had an enjoyable time. It was a different spiritual path but one of self-disrupt and self-sabotage to block out painful emotions. I still listen to rave music but use mind memory like you use muscle memory with exercise. I have a very vivid and vast imagination. Nothing that I do is scripted and goes very much on the energy.

Reiki and Storytelling

Reiki 11 was fascinating as it was very multidimensional. You could send the Reiki back in time and across time. As a little girl, I would always be gazing up at the sky and thinking there is more out there. I got a real fascination with quantum physics, which I detail later in the book. One of the exercises was to send Reiki to one of the other students, and they had to give feedback on when you were sending and what they were feeling. What I love about Reiki is that it is very hands-on and highly creative. I also sent it to friends, and they gave me feedback about what they felt. When it was time to compare notes, the results matched. It was so amazing. Back then, the symbols were sacred and only shared between the students from the Reiki Master. It was very much watching and feeling. Listen to your hands. Reiki is remarkably simple, and you follow your intuition. You are a healer and a channel, so you are not using your energy. You are using the Universal life force energy.

After about a year, I wanted to learn more about Reiki, so I asked Gary for some help. He said he was no longer teaching and going on a different path but saw how ready I was to learn more and go far with Reiki. He advised me to join the Reiki Association, of which I have been a member now for 19 years. I joined and had no idea what to expect. I went to my very first Annual Reiki Gathering at Buckland Hall, an exceptionally beautiful mansion in The Brecon Beacon and would become my spiritual home for the next few years.

During this gathering is where I got adopted by Louisa Booth. I was one of the only people at the Gathering without a Master and had someone making a bit of a dig, and she was so full of shit. Not one to mince my words even back then. I was one of the youngest at the gathering but made quite an impression. The late Paul Mitchel spoke, and I put my hand up and said, I do not know what you are talking about. People looked at me, thinking, oh shit, he is not one to upset. He was totally cool.

I got people coming up to me afterwards saying that you were only asking what we wanted to say and dare not ask. I never got this as I am an only child, so I was fearless in many ways. I got called cocky at an interview. That was more of a defence as I built this feistiness to cover up the 'are you for real.' For every job I wanted to do, I got told I cannot do that. So, I was a bit cocky when I went for a YTS Care Assistant job. I was a bit of a rebel at times. I could stick up for myself and have always been a very hard worker. I am very polite, and I do know how to behave. Well, most of the time. I am just me.

Back to Louisa Booth. She found me refreshing and fascinating and took me under her wing. Louisa lived in London and invited me to my first ever Reiki Share. I had never been to one before and was blown away. I had seven people giving me Reiki at the same time. I was floating on air for days and was hooked—a natural drug, naturally high. I am still running Reiki Shares 19 years later.

My lovely London Reiki Share group are still wonderful friends, and they are always there for me when I need them and vice versa. They also joined me as part of the Wellbeing Network. You cannot build these connections online. Throughout the pandemic, we have been running online Reiki shares. It was not quite the same but was powerful. Reiki has kept many of us sane and connected in the pandemic. It also kept us strong to send healing to the front-line workers and the situation. We lightworkers are the silent army.

I learned so much working alongside Louisa and eventually retrained with her. I felt the Reiki energy much stronger. Wanya attuned Louisa, and I was totally mesmerised by her presence and storytelling. I feel so privileged to have met both Wanya and Phyllis. I warmed up to Wanya the most. They were both different, and I warmed more to Phyllis in her later years and felt she was much happier. I was mesmerised watching Wanya give a live Reiki treatment at one of the gatherings in the same way as she was taught by Mrs. Takata, the Grandmaster and a living legend who brought Reiki to the West.

Girl power at its finest. A tiny lady with a massive why. Without Mrs. Takata, you would not be reading this book. She connected so many people and changed so many people's lives. I am passing on the legacy that she learned from Dr. Usui. Learning from the source at such a close level is especially important to me. I love reading, but to meet these legends in the flesh was truly priceless. Because I have met them and connected with them, I can bring them into my practice and channel them into the sessions I run. I feel their presence very clearly.

I feel compelled to give these beautiful souls justice and follow the Reiki tradition in a pure form; this does not mean living like a nun or a saint, but it does mean that I live to the highest good of all. You have a gift that can only be used for good. It is a gift, and you need to treat it with the respect it truly deserves and not mess with it.

I went on a fantastic journey with Louisa Booth, and we created our legacy. We started running courses together. I was on my Reiki Master training apprentice, which gave me years of massive growth. I did not realise I was on the Reiki Master apprentice path; as such, it evolved in the right divine timing. The leadership qualities and my organisational and networking skills were a natural progression. It was 12 years later when I did finally become a Reiki Master. Not with Louisa, though, as we lived a long way apart, and money was very tight for me as a single mum to travel.

I carried on the tradition and brought Reiki Shares with me to Grimsby through the local Reiki experience group where a beautiful lady June ran the service for the local community hub. It took awhile to establish them, and they were more Reiki experience days and not ones just for Reiki practitioners themselves. I loved having and giving Reiki to people who already had Reiki. It is also great for when you are not feeling well enough to give Reiki treatments to the general public. Reiki Shares are the Reiki Association's embodiment, which provides life to the community.

It was not for me, though, as I was not strong enough at this time to give Reiki to the general public and wanted to heal myself first. Years of working with disadvantaged groups had taken their toll on my own health, and I had a lot of healing work to do on myself. I started to do small Reiki Shares in my new home. Two of the ladies, Angela and Adele from June's group, decided they would like to come to a share just for them. They loved it. I later met Tracy Kelly at a meeting run by Anne Winslow, who runs beautiful healing sessions. I went to Anne a few times to help with my healing.

Tracy is a Reiki Master and had moved from out of town, so we had lots in common. Fitting into town life after travelling and moving from a big city can be extremely hard. It is a slower pace of life. Tracy started coming to my shares, and I started running Reiki tea and chat groups at different local independent cafes around Grimsby and Cleethorpes. I joined an in-walk innovation with Adam Shaw in London, which was all about walking and healing, so I arranged local Reiki walks and picnics.

Tracy met Angela and Adele, and we had lots of beautiful Reiki Shares. We all had vastly different journeys into Reiki, so it was amazing to blend in the experience. I started to feel stronger and was ready to become a Reiki Master. I had done all the training, so I was ready to take it to the next level and become a teacher. Tracy said she would run a course; Angela and Adele also wanted to become Reiki Masters. We all had different routes we wanted to go on. I was told you will be on one hell of a rollercoaster once you decide to take that final leap. This is one of the reasons I do not teach courses online, as I want to be fully there for my students.

What is remarkably interesting is Tracy does teach online as she has come down a different path. Tracy gets on amazingly well with teaching Reiki online and has an international following. It was a great learning for Tracy to see how I had been taught Reiki and how I ran Reiki courses. Tracy had a manual to give to her students. I tried to make one, but this did not work for me. I am very hands-on, and the videos work well for me. I want to be able to get my students going on to get very hands-on.

In my Reiki Master group, we are all so different. Tracy is very much into healing for animals, uses a lot of crystals, and created Angle Palm Beads. She is also training to be a psychologist. Angela decided her journey was to go more into the meditation side, and Adele wanted to enhance her practice. I was so ready to go out there and teach Reiki. I had been training for this for 15 years before becoming a master.

Reiki has no right or wrong way, and some people want to do all three levels very quickly. I would not recommend that, but this is not my path. I give any students that come to me the tools to find their path, and I am there as a guide and ready to aid them on their journey. I have six students, and one lovely lady, Yvonne, is on her Reiki Master journey with me. She has blossomed and is a beautiful, gifted healer. Every journey is so magical and special. Some students stay at Reiki 1 and that is perfectly okay.

The friendships you make with Reiki are incredibly special. We are all connected, and Reiki connects you on a deeper soul level.

Reiki is not all love and light

Reiki is not all love and light and gentle healing; it will and does bring up your shit. I never gloss things over and explain the dark shadow side to everyone I teach and share Reiki with. People need to be prepared for anything that comes up. Reiki gives you what you need and not what you think you want. For example, somebody may come to you with a backache. The backache is only a symptom, and you may get an emotional release instead of a physical one. Back is often money worries, stored anger and resentment, and not moving forward. I can go very deep into this as there is so much to what the body is telling you. I will recommend my favourite book instead, which I mentioned before, "You Can Heal Your Life" by the legendary Louise Hay. It was because of her teaching that I followed the Reiki path.

Chapter 4

Becoming a Leader, The Wellbeing Network Years.

This business is my baby and I have many goals I have wanted to achieve for a long time. One is to become a global motivational speaker. I started my YouTube channel in 2010, but I put this outlet on hold whilst surviving as a single mum, and I restarted again during the global pandemic.

Before all of this, when I was in London, I was invited to be a Life Wheel Leader to run a Wellbeing Network, about 2008. I was a true leader when I ran the team set up by Neil Davidson, a very respected businessman who became my mentor and friend. He believed in me and helped me develop my elevator pitch and push forward as a businessperson, leader, and influencer. I wanted to inspire others. I had no clue about being a leader and why I was picked as a leader back then. This was a lie that I was telling myself. I was leading long before this.

Nobody told me that I was not particularly good as an only child, and I developed lots of confidence as I had no sibling rivalry. Many natural-born leaders are only children.

This was not the first time, it often happened, but I did not feel worthy of being a leader. I know now why this is, and it is now known as imposter syndrome. Being told I was useless and thick often had cut deep, affecting my self-belief, confidence, and self-esteem. It was buried deep in the unconscious mind, and there was always a thought that I was going to be found out very soon, and it will all come crashing down, and people will see I am not that good and just acting the part to please others. Yes, another symptom of this is people-pleasing ways.

I grew up watching others as I did not know how to follow conversations and act in the so-called normal way. It took time and practice. This was not easy. I now make it seem so natural, and I am no longer acting, and I am myself. It is so freeing, and I no longer feel exhausted after being with people. I was striving to be perfect and people-pleasing. This cut deep and festered into every pour of my essence. I did not know how to cure this, and you do not know what you do not know. Until I started reading about this everywhere. When you are ready, you are put on the path to help you to overcome the lesson.

We keep repeating the same lessons until we utterly understand them and accept that this is a lesson coming up to be healed. When you realise this, lessons can come thick and fast, and you think at times can you let me off the treadmill please, and you can go on one hell of a bumpy ride that is not pretty, and you can lose a lot of people along the way. This was the Law of Attraction starting to unfold. I was now aware that my thoughts were becoming a reality and that I needed to find a way to help my thoughts to become more positive. The power of the mind is the only thing that matters. Working with people who did not have a fully functioning body but still had a powerful mind, I saw that they were so much more blessed. Many of my clients lost their minds due to dementia, Alzheimer's, depression, or many other illnesses related to the mind.

I always had this thing in the back of my head that I would be found out and wanted to know when things would get easier and not have that old program running around deep in my unconscious mind. Despite this, I cracked on and put on a smile and did my best. I met the most amazing people back in 2006, and most are still in touch to this day and truly have my back as I will always have their back. I will never forget those who have seen me at my worst and still supported me. It is so easy for many just to see the successful you. The long hard roads to success are a hugely different story. I would not change it as it has created a strong leader that everybody else could see. I needed to learn to feel and believe it myself.

I met many of these amazing people via Ecademy, the brainchild of Thomas and Penny Power. Such an amazing couple and well ahead of their time. They built Ecademy before LinkedIn was born. They had a vision of building a community of like-minded visionaries and entrepreneurs. I loved going to the monthly meetings at Victoria. I had only just started my business then, and all I had was a Reiki table and a massive vision to fulfil. It was only later the full rewards started to come into place.

Like many other business owners, I have ridden the storms and the hardships along with the buzz of the amazing highs. Being an entrepreneur certainly keeps you on your toes which is always a bonus for a tiny 5 foot 2 single mum. I did not know at the time that I would be teaching people to elegantly stand on their toes with elegance, ease, and grace once I became a Pilates Teacher and a pioneer for the neurodiversity and disability sectors.

I watched the great leaders every spare moment and was learning how the great speakers move, stand, speak, and hold the audience. I learned how they loop the stories to capture you in building you up and capturing your emotional essence. This world opened for me, and I was well and truly ready. Well not quite; I had many big boulders to smash through on the long twisting roads to acceptance. The universe had other plans for me first.

Whilst this was happening, I was losing more and more interest in my day job. Getting into trouble as I had lost my passion for it. Burnout and stress had sucked the life out of me. This new world was lifting me; spending this time with happy, driven, and hungry, motivated beings uplifted me.

They believed in me, so why the struggle with believing in myself. I was not used to being told I was awesome and a great leader. I was so used to only being pulled up for what I had done wrong. The last few years of my working life, I did just as much as I needed to keep my job to pay the bills and stay afloat until I could leave. I was not staying until I retired as many left with ill health or did not make retirement. I wanted my health back and to live an amazing life in fantastic health. There was no point staying to get a pension if I was not going to be around to enjoy it.

We were like a family, so watching your friends get sicker and sicker and stressed was so hard. The cuts were brutal. I started to reserve my energy for building a new life for myself as I was ready to take that leap into the unknown. It was a calculated leap as I had a good salary, a massive mortgage, and loads of debts. I was not sure how it would happen, but was very much into the Law of Attraction, which is where I went next.

Through the lovely well-being network, I met more and more people and got invited to lots of motivational seminars and events. I had recently watched the Secret and got an invite to a three-night Seminar with Dr. Demartini from the Secret. I was fascinated by him as he is a well-published author and motivational speaker. He talked about quantum physics and was speaking to my soul. I understood this language. The written word was never my thing, but energy is. He also looked at the spitting image of my stepfather, to whom I looked up. He was an exceedingly kind, respectable man who showed me how a true gentleman treats ladies. He had old-school manners and was always very well presented.

Dr. Demartini talked fast, and he moved fast, and he tapped into my amazingly fast and expansive hunger for knowledge. When I had spoken in the past that I had dyslexia, I had many individuals start to talk slowly to me and say bless you, and I just went into screensaver mode and just switched off to them. Someone often mistakenly told me I was not paying attention or being disrupted or lazy.

Nope, I was bored and not interested in the slightest. I learned over time to behave and look as if I was interested. If I were interested, then I would be fully engaged. I often got told I was a great actor at work, and I had to fit in. The real me had not had the adaptations fitted so that I could truly thrive and shine brightly. I was exhausted just trying to be so-called normal. They call it masking now. I have struggled following conversations as a child. I am not sure how many labels I would have if I were diagnosed now.

Back to Dr. Demartini. He was vast and fast and wrote hundreds of books, and he also had dyslexia. In this new world, I met more and more talented fellow dyslexics. All I had faced so far was bless and let me fix you. I was in the healing world, which used to piss me off. I did not want to be fixed. I loved being me, and this was a part of me. I wanted to explore this beautiful part of me. I had never been in the right environment. There is no disability if you are in the right place. It is only the restrictions that we have supporting us.

I see the same questions pop up in my son's head all the time. He comes home drained for a school day, and he is in one of the better ones. He is in a Total Immersive School. So, it is fully interactive. Who decided that sitting at a desk for hours on end was the best way to learn? Does one size fit all? I question everything. These seminars blew my mind; they were fun, interactive, and immersive. I did not know back then that I would become an Immersion Wellbeing Coach. I bloody well-earned it, that is for sure. Blood, sweat, and tears to pass my exams in a world that was not equipped for us gifted neurodiverse talented, sensitive, and true genius expansive brains. Without this out-of-the-box thinking, we would still be thinking the world was flat. We think so far outside the proverbial box that it can scare many, including ourselves. We see things in minute details that others will not even think about.

I was often told to shut up and listen. I was not one to do as I was told and would keep asking questions and call people out on their bullshit. I would ask questions that many would want to ask but were afraid to look stupid. I was used to being told I was stupid, so it got to the point that I was not bothered.

Quite often, the person shutting me down looked more stupid than me. Many of those are running the country or telling us how to live. I shut my mind off to those individuals and make a difference in my way. When I have been quiet, these have been my most dangerous times. These have been when I have been growing and working out better ways of being. I have had lots of people try to shut me up and take me down over the years, but I am no quitter.

One thing many people say about me is my tenacious nature of never giving up when many would have given up or never even started. Why do I keep going? My Why is bigger than myself, and we are not here for long, and we all want to leave a legacy. Why would I choose the most difficult way for me to get my true message out there? The written word is not my first language. Audio is. I want to show that you can put your mind to anything you set your attention on. If I help one person see their vision and inspire them, this little vision of mine will not be wasted. We are always learning and evolving.

Not quite ready for the big stage

Not all the events went to plan. I went with an incredibly special gentleman called Adam Shaw. We met at an Annual Reiki Gathering in Buckland Hall in Wales. We were drawn to each other to bring out each other's lessons and fast. Some people come into your life and get you to your vision much faster. Adam was one of those people. We certainly had many adventures and misadventures.

We got tickets for a Chris Howard Seminar over at Alexander Palace. It was long sessions over the three days, so Adam booked a room above a pub close by. It was basic and had shared bathrooms and toilets. There were lots of people staying there and close to the seminar. Living in London, it was still the norm to book a hotel if you travelled on weekends due to road works and lack of transport.

The excitement was building for this seminar, and I had no idea what to expect. Thousands of people in one place. We shared a room. Adam went to use the facilities, and I also went to use the facilities. I went in with just my towel. Neither of us had taken a key. Well, the drama unfolded. The owner was off-premises, and there I was standing in this tiny towel and nothing underneath. Adam was not impressed, and a crowd was starting to gather. I looked in the next room to see if I could climb on the ledge and clamber into a window. I had seen it in plenty of movies.

It was a very slim ledge, and I was in my towel. I didn't even have tomorrow's washing on. Sharon Stone, I was not. I came back in and looked at the lock. It did not look too strong, and I was into Kung Fu. So, I asked everyone to move back, did a high kick, and kept my modesty in check. The door opened. I then went ahead to fix the lock with my keys. Adam was mortified and called me a scallywag for being able to fix the lock. I come from a humble background and have a bit of scallywag in me. I still to this day drink lager from a can. I do love champagne from a fancy flute, though.

The drama was over, and we went to the Chris Howard Event. Adam had enough of my drama, so he went and sat away from me. We were very separate individuals, so we wanted to fully immerse ourselves in this event. I went to see Adam at the interval, and news had spread. I was getting I do not recognize you with your clothes on. I was born for the stage, but this was not how I wanted to achieve it but what a story to tell the grandkids and make others laugh.

I had many more misadventures with Adam, but that would be another book. One involved a tiny English brolly and big boulders of ice rain on a Greek mountain. The said word was can things get any worse. The heavens truly opened and Adam sang singing in the rain. What a site that was. At least thousands of people never witnessed that one.

The friendships I have made from the Wellbeing Network are friends for life. I asked myself three questions when I was looking for people to join me on my life wheel, which the Wellbeing Network was all about. It is small community hubs making a significant difference and finding others who share your vision. I learned early on that it takes an idea to make a difference and start a movement. Then the seeds are planted, and it starts to grow roots. This foundation level was the making of my life and business. The same concept of it takes a community to bring up a child.

What were the three questions you may ask?

I had long thought about this and worked out I had spent years working for or under people I did not like or respect. Most of my colleagues I loved and respected, and it was the suits and the higher management that I did not respect. So, I thought a lot about this one. These are what I came up with.

Question 1 - Could I go on holiday with this person?

Question 2 - Do I feel energised and light when I am around this person?

Question 3 - Do they share the same vision, values, and beliefs that there is a higher purpose in life than just paying the bills and living for the weekends?

I was not looking for team members that were too hippy-dippy or up in the air. I was looking for ambitious, passionate, forward-thinking visionaries who wanted to make a difference in the world. There was no agenda on race, cultural diversity, sexuality, or levels of wealth, and I wanted us all to share the same passion. Like I said before, we were way ahead of our time, just like Ecademy, which came before LinkedIn.

Neil set me up on my leadership training, and he got me practising my elevator pitch. We did lots of role-playing, and he guided me every step of the way. Through the networking, at Ecademy I met my team members - Mel, Alison, Diana, Sandra, Devan, and Ntathu. Then Karen who later married Devon.

Deven found a beautiful meeting venue, which was a Vegan Caribbean Diner. Not trendy back then, but we were all into plant-based soul food, and this was perfect - healthy juices, the best vegan mac and cheese, and a fantastic vibe.

This is where our shared vision was born.

The beautiful Mrs. M (Matanah) ran the diner and wrote an amazing Vegan Caribbean cookbook, which is proudly displayed on my bookcase. About 90% of us from this group are authors and successful to this day. We are not successful in the so-called traditional sense with big mansions, walk-in wardrobes and university education. Not that there's anything wrong with this. I love my shoes and beautiful things as much as everyone else.

Why are we so successful? It is because we are the glue to the community, know we can phone each other up in times of crisis, and we have a trusted unbreakable bond. In this fast and vast social media world, this is priceless, especially in this cancel-out culture. We had that strong offline organic bond first. The internet was about to explode, but we were connected in the flesh. It was a well-being hub for vibrant souls to share music, stories, culture, and art plus the blessed food made with love.

This is where we planned our well-being events. We did a lot of trial events as there was not a lot of this about back in the 2000s. It was very corporate. Reiki was not even recognized as a real therapy either. Not that any of this stopped us. On this life wheel, I needed to find like-minded holistic therapists from different disciplines - mine was Reiki; Mel was Reiki and Massage; Alison was Personal Training, body balance, Reiki, and Nutrition; Ntathu was Yoga, mindfulness, and meditation, plus an author; Deven a massage therapist and many other therapies; Sandra Couples Counselling coach, massage and so many other talents; Diana the Founder of Habit Breakers and loads of disciplines from Hypnotherapy, stopping smoking services, NLP and so much more. None of us was getting paid to do this and it was all voluntary until we eventually started to expand on it all.

Through this beautiful space, Melanie was having a catch-up and a smoothie when a tiny little soul came down to visit us. She was only two years old and kept insisting her mum come downstairs to meet us. This little girl is not little anymore and is an entrepreneur and an extraordinarily talented young lady. Her Mummy is the beautifully talented Marcia, singer, songwriter, and Sound Healer. Our paths began to cross more and more, and Marcia and Anya came to a small taster event that we organised.

We were meant to meet, and Anja knew this. She is a pure gifted soul. I was offering free taster Reiki sessions and Marcia had some Reiki from me. It was a short session, but it was deep, and I needed to leave not long afterwards to get some air. I had not learned to fully ground myself at this point and this healing went on to a very deep level for Marcia. She reported back to me that she felt amazing and went into detail about her story. We are still soul sisters to this day. Another unbreakable bond.

Marcia went on to organise a sound healing and holistic therapy event. We were all part of this beautiful day. This was my very first event where I was the guest speaker. I got a lot of constructive criticism, which was the beauty of the team. I was still building up my confidence here. I told my Reiki story. Little did I know back then that I was destined to be on the stage as an international motivational speaker and a pioneer in my industry. I had one of the guys at the event say that I needed to practice speaking more and could tell I was new to it. I took his advice on board and started to practice.

Success does not happen overnight. When people say you were an overnight success it is very rarely the case. When you become an expert in your field it is because you have been continuous with your daily actions. Tiny actions over a lengthy period accumulate over time. These can be good or bad. The Late Great Jim Rohn once said if you ate a chocolate bar instead of an apple every day, then you would see an accumulation of health issues from eating a daily chocolate bar. The saying goes that you can't out-train a poor diet.

During a lockdown, my old beliefs started to rear their ugly head again. So, I got down to pen and paper and this is my free flow letting go exercise. I have regular twice-monthly coaching which got me through lockdown and kept my business ticking over. This is what I wrote.

I am enough, I put myself first, I am ready to give up my people-pleasing ways. I deserved to be cherished, nurtured, valued and loved. Lockdown had been an emotional roller coaster and a mind muck. So many emotions, so much judgement. So many gifts inside the madness. Having lovely healing sessions from all the beautiful authors in my first co-authored book Wild Women Rising gave me time to reflect, slow down and take stock. The wound on my chest is ready to burst out and let out all the negative crap. A year earlier this manifested into the physical form and had a very nasty infection bursting out of my chest. I am ready to let go of the limiting beliefs that stop me from moving forward. The low-level energy will shift and I will feel light and free again. Ready to step into the person that I was born to be. Thank you Thank You Thank You and so it is.

Chapter 5

The Travel and Adventure Years

Living in London in the 1990s was a life of freedom, partying, and excess. I had a comment from my yoga teacher who had me working out. She said you are never truly present in class until a Wednesday night. She knew me too well. I worked hard and partied even harder. I lived for the weekends and danced the night away. Drink, raving, and dance. She knew she could not stop me from being a party animal and being self-destructive, but she could help me to keep some sort of normality and damage limitation. This felt like my spiritual home for a few years. A place to escape.

I lived for holidays, travelling to faraway destinations off the beaten track. A time when there were no selfies and just a chance to just be and have an enjoyable time. One of the most amazing places I have ever been to is Goa in India. It was a place of true poverty and colour at the same time. I love the culture and the vibrancy. I was single and very much on the journey of self-discovery. A lovely lady I met through the Wellbeing Network agreed to go with me.

We did not know each other very well. She said if we have separate huts, red wine, and yoga she was in.

We arrived jet-lagged in the middle of the night, and ready to discover India. It was a full moon. We had a few drinks and eventually went to bed. I was in a dream-like state. People were jumping in the sea naked. Two men were watching from behind a boat. We looked at them and said that is not going to be us.

A mixture of alcohol and jet lag, plus lack of sleep. All I could hear were the waves. I remember thinking I needed to switch the tape off as the waves were so loud. I then realised that I was living on Palolem Beach in a beach hut. I was posh and had a flushing toilet. No shower but very privileged to have a proper toilet. I drifted back to sleep to the beautiful sounds of the sea. This was home for the next three weeks.

It took a few days to truly relax into Indian life. Paula and I would meet at sunset every day for a cup of herb tea or a cocktail and watch the beautiful kaleidoscope of colours as the sun descended on the sea. This is how I have created many of my mindfulness meditations. None of which have been copied from a book but purely from my vivid imagination. One of the many gifts of my neurodiverse brain.

Yoga in India was amazing. I met a lovely lady called Loren who had such beautiful energy. We would practice yoga in a beautiful open-air space full of natural beauty. Nothing beats doing yoga in its place of birth. I went on to do another one of her beautiful retreats in Turkey, in the amazing mountains of Fethiye.

I had the most amazing ayurvedic massages, which were in very rustic huts. I met a kindred soul called Raj who was on the same wavelength as myself. He was so humble, and we talked about the real stuff. He left his family for a few months every year to support his family. I gave him business advice and got him to create a guest book and write down how they found his massages. He was so humble and grateful for this. I had full-body massages, ayurvedic massages, and full aromatherapy massages. I felt very safe and at ease in his presence.

I did, unfortunately, get very badly bitten at one stage and my bite was infected. I visited the local ayurvedic clinic and they said it was one of the worst infections that they have seen. I went for daily treatment and thankfully I was ok and ended up with no scar. I was told I have sweet blood. I still suffer very badly with bites and need to be incredibly careful. I had the same issue in Guyana and in Greece. It was a blessing and I make sure I have full medical cover wherever I travel. Tiny insects love me.

During my daily yoga practice, I had this little ant join me on my yoga mat. He was a beautiful little soul and would stretch with me. In this fast go - go - go society we do not notice such beautiful blessings. I see ants as the silent army who scurry away going about their business and making sure things run smoothly in the background. I never take nature for granted and these little creatures are an especially important part of this ecosystem.

One day out we decided to go to a secluded beach. Another beautiful soul took us on his boat. He said he will pick us up later. We decided to get a taxi home. He waited and waited for us. We did not find out until the next day.

We felt so bad as he would work so hard and did not own the boat. He earned so little to support his family. We went to find him to apologise, and he invited us back to his family home. A small home with very few home comforts. We were so grateful he had invited us into his humble home.

A friend we met in India bought him the boat and we set him up on a mobile phone contract. He was not fully set up in business and able to support his family. He was so grateful, and tears welled up in his eyes. He never expected such generosity from us, but to us it was such a small gesture. To this day I am grateful for the privileged life that I lead.

On this very same trip, they were organising a boat trip. The group asked if I was coming as they found out I was into sailing. I looked at the sky and said no way. They looked at me puzzled and said the weather is beautiful. I am particularly good at reading the sky and said there is no way I am going out. A few hours later they all came back extremely sick and traumatised. The storm was brutal. I was sitting in a hammock and the rain started and I had to run up lots of steps to my wooden mountain hut. They were looking at me when they came back as if to say we wish we listened to you.

Even in the lean periods, I have never been at that level of poverty. When staying in Guyana, we paid 50 dollars to set up a family with a water system. I also pay for a young lady in the Gambia to go to school and get regular reports on her progress. She is about 14 now. My son said he would love a sister and the opportunity to sponsor a young girl. I will always be giving back, no matter how small.

My son, Benjamin, is growing up to be a grateful young man. When he sees homeless people, he always wants to give. We were in London once and a young homeless lady brought his coat out that he left in a café. He has so much time for everyone. He knows he has a privileged life even though we do not always have a lot left after the bills are paid. He knows that if the fridge is full then we are very blessed.

I want to travel the verandas of the world, writing and sketching. I sat sketching in Guyana. This was a fascinating place as I was the only white person in the area where I was staying. I watched the beautiful children going to school every day from the veranda and they would stop and look at me and buy things from the shop below. The talking went up whilst I was there. I loved listening to the sounds of the jungle and listening to nature. I even got catapulted by frogs one night during a storm. I was there during the rainy season. It was still baking hot and got blisters on my back in the shade sitting under a coconut tree sketching.

I have never been into fad diets or detoxing

I went back to one of Loren's retreats and she was doing a detox alongside the yoga and massages. She said it will be an extra £50 a week. My unfiltered response was why would I want to pay extra money to eat virtually nothing. I watched the detox group get more and more miserable. I enjoyed the beautiful fresh plant-based diet that was supplied every day. I was not going to miss the beautiful food. Even back in the 1990s, I was a lot curvier than most yogis. I did not care as I have always loved my food and was not going to miss such beautiful fresh food. Cooking food, eating food, growing food and shopping for food is still a great passion of mine. My clients are always in for a treat when I run workshops and courses.

This leads me to why I stopped giving dietary advice in Lockdown. I was putting lots of energy into doing posts about nutrition and living a more plant-based chemical reduced diet. I would put in a lot of effort and people would ignore my advice and just go to pages that had lost ten pounds in a week. I got fed up and decided to stop. I will teach nutrition and go through this with one-to-one clients but only clients who are truly ready to listen. When you have diabetic nurses telling your diabetic mother that sweeteners are ok, then I am fighting a losing battle. I kept saying you are better off not using anything.

I tried a very well known protein shake that's vegan. They put sweetener in it. I said why did you have to put it in the shake, why can you not just have a separate sachet for those who do not want it in the shake. They said I was the only one going on about this and that the general public needed the sweetness. The coffees are now so sweet that they taste disgusting. I have sent so many coffees back. You are better off with black coffee and cream. All this banging on about low fat when the coffee industry is serving drinks with double the calorie intake of say porridge or Weetabix.

I saw the obesity crisis unfolding back in early 2000. I authored my essays on it for my Diploma in Health and Social welfare. The demise started to happen when the High Street was on the decline and the big supermarkets opened. Many could only be reached by car, so we were no longer walking and buying much more than we needed.

When I was at school in the 1970s and 1980s there were few ready meals, and most meals were made from fresh local ingredients that were in season. Now we have so much non-food in supermarkets and live in a ding society. Two minutes in the microwave and no interaction. Food was always a social activity bringing the family together. We may live in the same house now, but you might not see each other. Some families text each other in the house.

We even have several bins outside our houses for all the plastic waste. If you shopped locally and cooked from scratch, then we would not have so much plastic waste. Even boiled eggs are in the shops ready-made and packaged in plastic. Why not just cook loads of eggs at once and take them to work? When did life get so busy that you do not have time to boil a few eggs? I went very much on a tangent then, but it is the trivial things that make a massive difference. Not a load of suits flying off to sort out climate change. That defeats the object. It starts with you.

You may be thinking about what this has to do with the travel years. It has everything to do with the travel years as it opened my eyes to what is important.

I went to Cyprus four years ago and stayed in my friend's lovely villa. There was the annual festival on and the whole square was full of music, families of all generations of families all coming together and sharing food, drinks, singing and laughter. We have lost that over the years and in a less developed country the village was more connected and happier. Even if money was short everyone pulled together and looked after each other.

Another observation. I have suffered from IBS since my late teens and when I went to Guyana and lived on fresh local produce, I had no symptoms. As soon as I got back to the UK all the symptoms came back. Even eating fruit and vegetables was causing me issues. By the time the fruit and veg get to the shops, it has already passed its best or pumped up full of chemicals or pollutants, not to mention the air miles. I have had fruit sit in the bottom of my fridge for months and it is still the same. Back in the 1970s, I would eat fruit straight away as it would deteriorate after a couple of days. To this day I advocate a chemical-free diet and still never count calories.

Living in London and travelling has enabled me to expand my palate and to relax, as I love to cook and share beautiful meals. Every event that I put on for people always has a food and drink element to it. For me, just turning up for a yoga class is not enough. I have always loved the community element. During my Iyengar Yoga years, we would all go to a vegan café near Deptford High Street. The Wellbeing Network meetings ran from a Vegan Caribbean Diner and Yin Yang was regular meals out around south London.

I am not vegan but did eat a lot of plant-based food as I was dairy-free for 20 years. I could not go vegetarian. I do eat meat but not very much and only from a particularly decent quality butcher. Eggs are also only from free-range or local farms. I also love olive oil and use that on my body to keep the engine running inside my body. I have been to Greece and Turkey many times and follow the Mediterranean diet as much as possible. I treat my body like a car. Putting in the best oil I can possibly find. I have had some stick over the years for not being vegan and a yogi but found the diet too restrictive when I am not able to tolerate a lot of the foods. I would never eat junk food or vegan food. It is so easy to cook vegan food with imagination, herbs, and spices.

This leads me onto the network marketing years and the wonderful product that I started to use.

Chapter 6

When the comfort zone no longer feels comfortable, you need to get the hell out.

Despite all the Reiki and the yoga and all the Wellbeing learnings, I was struggling and could no longer keep the mask on, and everything fell apart. Sometimes we need to have a massive forest fire to clear the debris that forces us to start again. It is so unbelievably difficult when you are going through the dark night of the soul. One on the other side you see the true blessings and beauty of what you went through.

Living with the long-term effects of Chronic Stress and Burnout

My situation became harder in care work and I suffered from burnout and signed off for six weeks due to stress. My boss told me that the break would not look good for future employment. But I was never employed again and do not ever intend to be. Well, not in the traditional sense.

I had the worst burnout this time. I could not even go to the gym, which had always been my go-to. I slept a lot and went for a daily walk. I would walk to the library and spend some time there. I was getting to know my local area for the very first time. I had been on this hamster wheel for years, going fast and never having time to smell the flowers. I walked to my local park and sat in a tree to think. I started to rewrite my journal. Something that I had stopped doing.

I went back after six weeks on light duties but was still very fragile. I had an incident and ended up on my second disciplinary. During this time, I hit the Fuck it switches and thought about why I should behave myself and be the model employee. I started to go out more, party more and start drinking. I have never been a big drinker as I had liver problems in my twenties so it was recommended to not drink. This stuck with me, and I never really missed out. I did not recognize myself during this period, but my life was a mess. I wanted out from my job, my life as it was, and things got very dark and messy.

Then in the middle of all of this, I discovered I was pregnant. I thought I was too old and going through early menopause. Two disciplinary notes had to be put on the back burner as they cannot sack a pregnant woman. I may have been a cat in a past life as I have been given many lifelines. My main concern now was getting extremely healthy and planning my new chapter. The fighter in me kicked in. If I was going to be sacked or put onto the capability road, then I was not going without a proper fight or a big send-off. I had worked as a carer for over 20 years and my future was not being taken away due to austerity and cuts.

The good that came out of my break was that I was sent on some extra training as I could no longer cope with my dyslexia and burnout. Due to cuts and austerity, I was called on to do things at the very last minute. I later found out that this is not something I can deal with easily and need time to plan and process. My bosses just thought I was being difficult and being a diva. I had a further assessment from the Dyslexia Institute in Kennington. There, I was diagnosed with dyspraxia, which is difficulty in processing information and problems with sequencing and balance. It was a very productive time. I got my diagnosis at Access to Work and finding out about dyspraxia was amazing. Liz Gentilcore was a Neurodiversity consultant for the Dyslexia Institute in Kensington. I was 38 when diagnosed, whilst I was pregnant.

This diagnosis was such a relief and explained why I struggled to process information. It had been exhausting trying to live in a system that was not fully structured to my individual needs. Ramps were made if you were in a chair but if you had any mental health issues or were not fully being the model employee of ticking the so-called boxes then you were seen as not being fit for purpose. So, the pattern was happening again. I could no longer be in this place and knew I needed to get the hell out.

Many thought I was being a diva or difficult and lazy. Even to this day, some of my old colleagues said I only did as much work as I had to. This was so not true. I had to work extra hard just to do normal tasks and having a set routine really helped and not having bosses change things continually. I needed continuity just like my clients did. Fitting into a system that is not meant for you became unbearable. Anxiety, stress, not being able to function started to manifest into the physical body - joint pains, numbness and never feeling rested. The malaise got harder to walk through. My days became existence and I just went throughout the day like a zombie. I had fully lost all colour from my life - no more high definition, but rather just working to pay the bills and the debts with nothing to look forward to.

I was in the job I had always loved and still loved, but knew I needed to make changes or I would not fulfil my potential and needed to spread my wings. I did not know how, when, or why at this point, but that vision and self-belief that something bigger than myself was about to evolve. I realised it was time to be done with social care and start a new chapter. I was massively in debt, pregnant with a mortgage, and about to leave a secure and steady job. I was scared and excited about becoming a mother.

I worked up until the very last minute, so I could have my full maternity leave and have more time to plan my next steps. I left myself just two weeks before my due date. I was on light duties at this stage anyway, and due to being on a couple of disciplines, I was not able to do most of my duties anyway so I thought I may as well work for as long as I could. I was hoping things worked out so that I would not have to go back. I knew the entire system was haemorrhaging money and time wastage in all the wrong places. I had been planning all my groups and ran them on zero budgets. The suits just wasted hundreds of thousands of pounds on a load of shit.

During my sessions, Liz gave me hope. She did a lot of assessments on me and as part of the package, I was given eight dyslexia strategy sessions to find out how I can manage my workload better. I was already efficient, but the paperwork side had become more overwhelming.

I use lots of the strategies to this day, and they do save me lots of time. One of the main ones was copying things from a chalkboard to paper. I have always found this a challenge, so I was told to take pictures instead. Camera phones had only just started to become extremely popular. Blackberries were the thing then and smartphones were starting to explode.

Next on the list were email systems. The reason I ended up on a disciplinary was that I had missed a vital email with a new procedure. I had missed the training. This vital email would have been an in-person training day, but due to cuts was sent out via email. I had been sick, so had missed the handover. I had a fantastic session on how to put all the emails into categories and how to bookmark them. All my files were put into folders and were all in easy-to-access places on the desktop.

I was given a few items that would help me to see the wording on the computer better. The software was called Read and Write Gold. You could change the background and the fonts to suit you. It also spoke out the words if you needed it. Phonics was one of the issues that were picked up in my dyslexia diagnosis. The lady had picked up that due to lots of hearing issues when I was younger, I had not picked up phonics very well. Audio learning is my preferred learning style to this day. When I am creating any of my content, I make sure I cover all four areas of learning as we are all different - kinesthetic, audio, visual, and written.

You have the audio learners who like me have that television in your head at high definition. I love reading and often get disappointed when seeing a book being made into a film as I have such a sharp vision of how I want it to be in my mind.

Visual learners learn better from watching and seeing. This is also an enormously powerful way for me to learn. I am a Reiki Master, and this was a perfect course for me as it was hands-on and very practical. There was no written work involved and you learned through practice and observation. This also blends beautifully into the Kinesthetic style of learning which uses your senses and touch. This suits many holistic therapists as you get to use your senses a lot. I learn from movement, smells, and music. Anything that will trigger the creative side of the brain.

Then you have the reading and writing learners who want a detailed account of what to learn and how to do formats. I love reading and this is often a misconception for people with dyslexia. I read a lot and love to learn. I was taught how to skim read at university and pick up the main body of academic studies. It is a bit like fast-forwarding the boring bits of a TV program. We are bombarded with information, so it is finding out how to draw out the information that you need. I organise my mind like this and put my mind into files and categories. Lots of copying and pasting and bringing the relevant information to the surface and putting the less relevant stuff into a filing cabinet.

I have created a meditation called "shed head." It is not its official name as the world still wants fancy labels for stuff. In my hometown, many people say my head is like a shed. Meaning it is full of clutter and crap. I go deep into this mediation and do a clutter clearing of the shed, which translates to your mind and you're clear out what no longer serves you. You then reorganise the shed, aka the head, as a beautiful new space for you to visit anytime you feel overwhelmed, anxious or stressed. It is only 11 minutes long and powerful healing meditation. I called it a simple healing meditation, but this is the concept behind it. I got called out on some of my names such as Stretch, and Sleep as opposed to calling it Restorative Yoga as I want the public to be able to understand the language.

High-Definition Gifts

Working as an NVQ assessor was a real revelation for me. The suits had created this learning for the workers but put it in fancy words. I changed the language to suit the workers and not the suits so that my students got what the course was about. I was able to cross-reference eight units just from one day of following a student around without even writing a single note. I had that beautiful HD television in my head picking up everything. I would then go and write it up in the suit's language. They did not realise that I had changed all the wording as I do not think they would have liked my method, but I got my students through the course. I never did it for them and would not pass those that did not put in the work. I often got asked why it took so long to get the students to pass some of the modules. I said I am not passing them until I am fully happy that they are competent. I was putting my signature on the student and if they messed up, then it was down to my training. I am a hard but fair taskmaster.

I have created a few meditations in which I use these methods to help others. When I was a care assistant, I had a client who had Alzheimer's and she was picked to be part of a study to find out which part of the brain is affected and how it affects the client's behaviour. I was asked to write down my observations over a prolonged period by the specialists at Kings College Hospital. I would. The sad thing was they could not analyse the data until the client died and they cut up the brain. This stuff still fascinates me to this day and I went on to learn more at university. I went deeper into this in my Diploma in Health and Social Welfare.

Slightly off subject, what pains me to this day is why are care assistants still paid minimum wage when it is a highly skilled job? We handled so much more than just emptying bedpans and personal care. It is a real privilege to be able to look after people and be emotional support for their families. We are trained to an extremely elevated level.

Writing about this hopefully helps to change a few people's minds and see that services-led industries do need to be paid for their true value. Not the pen pushers and suits, who do not know the full extent of the skill that is involved and how cuts created more costs in the long run. Without the hidden army of carers, low-paid home workers, and mainly women who are sandwiched between looking after young children and parents then the economy would collapse. You need people like me to speak out and be the change.

I was given an ergonomic assessment so that I had all the things that I needed. I had to do my own pregnancy risk assessment as I was the only one fully trained to do this. So, I gave myself regular breaks and went in a bit later and left a bit earlier. Peak times to travel were particularly challenging as nobody gave up the training space for me on the train despite having a bump on board badge. London can be a very selfish place.

I worked up to the very last moment and thought I was going to have a couple of weeks to myself before Benjamin arrived. I had a few treatments planned such as massages and reflexology and was hoping the cleaning urge would kick in. I finished work on Friday, had a reflexology session on Saturday, and then the labour kicked in on Sunday; he was born on Tuesday. So, no time to prepare. It was good in a way as I had no time to overthink.

I had a chilled out labour in the brand-new birthing Centre in Lewisham. I was classed as old to be having a first baby and was seen as a considerable risk to have a baby in a birth Centre as opposed to a hospital. I was extremely healthy and passed all the checks. It was only after the birth that I had lots of health issues - not due to pregnancy but years of stress from the job.

Chapter 7

Network Marketing and Personal Development

I enjoyed going to lots of different meetings and needed to find some diverse ways of earning an income if I was going to be leaving my job at some point, so the universe was sending people into my life fast. A lady came into the day centre to talk about some health and wellness products.

As I was running mainly health and wellbeing sessions, I was invited to facilitate this talk. This lady is Camalita, and she is now rich and successful. She has been featured in the best-selling book, "Think and Grow Rich for Women." She is a global ambassador, speaker, author, and motivation superstar. Camalita spoke with such passion and was very much on her way to finding her true passion. I joined her team, and this was my first dip in the water for joining a network marketing company. When I met her, she was building her empire mainly from her car and small flat at the time.

The Products were Mannatech wellness products, and they were amazing. My sluggishness was gone and I was starting to feel very well. I lost weight and I lost bloating and that burnout feeling was going. I had to get up and go back. I had a newfound zest for life. Camalita and her passion rubbed off on me. I did not sell much in this business, but I loved the products and continued to use them as I needed to stay well to study, work full-time and build a legacy. I even kept taking them well into my pregnancy. I had a nurse say that I was extremely healthy for a geriatric expectant mother, a term that really does not sound nice but is still used to this day.

Because I was 38 when I was pregnant, being able to be booked into the brand spanking new birthing sweet in Lewisham was unusual. This was not offered to many older mums as we are seen as a substantial risk. I wanted a natural birth and loved the idea of not having my baby in a hospital. I got my wish and we both were healthy.

This business gives me insight into money systems and how to build different income streams. I knew then that I needed to find a way to make money to keep from working hour for hour. I needed to do something as I had ended up in the pattern of debt many times - building things up and then it all came crashing down again. I was trying to catch the wave and felt like I kept missing it. This time I knew that I was fully riding the wave.

Being a sailor for many years, I realised that to move forward we do not go in straight lines of roads. To get from a to b or even z we can go the scenic route and learn the biggest lessons of our lives.

To get moving on a boat you would need to often travel back several times to move forward. I bet many of you can relate to these times when you felt like you were walking through molasses. My life was no longer about me but my unborn child. I needed to build security for him. Even before my son was born, I knew he was going to be a boy. I never had the test; I did not need to.

My son and I only spent seven weeks in London and then I moved up to my hometown of Grimsby for my maternity leave. My mum first met her one and only grandson Benjamin at seven weeks old.

I had decided that it was not practical going back to my job in London, so it was a fresh start. I rented out my London flat and had income from that and maternity pay. This took the pressure off for a while and I could enjoy some time off before getting back to work. I was still studying so had lots to keep me occupied. Moving, studying, and having a new baby was a lot. I failed my final exams in Advanced Anatomy and Physiology. I needed this to pass my diploma in Pilates which had taken me four years of studying. I struggled to get through A and P for the Gym Instructor Training and needed extra support. Future Fit, who I was training with, was the best training provider I have ever had.

They did everything they possibly could to get me through this exam, well above and beyond what they needed to do. I could not pass in the way that the exam was presented to me. I tried and tried. In the end, I had a face-to-face exam and my lovely tutor spoke the exams to me. She even acted the exams as I found explaining the muscles and movements extremely hard. I was allowed to walk around to think. I needed the words to come alive. She said I do not pick up double negatives and need the wording to be presented in a unique way.

This was something that I naturally did for my own students when I was an NVQ assessor. I adapted the course to the student and did not expect them to pass a course that they had no way of passing even though they were fully competent. I had some students who were fantastic at the course work but put them on the floor with real-life people and they did not have the people skills. It was extremely hard to pass them. I had one say I do not like talking to people. I was very blunt back then and said you are in the wrong job. I suggest you get a job in a laboratory of something where you do not have to interact with people.

Luckily, I passed as this wonderful lady saw how good I was at teaching Pilates and saw me struggle through the Exercise to Music exams and she had every faith in me. I just needed that extra support. I will be forever grateful to her and the team at Future Fit. I passed GP and Exercise Referral and Pre and Post Natal Fitness on my second attempt. This is when people started to say to me that they would have given up. I had no choice. I had put four years into this, and I loved teaching. I needed that bit of paper to be fully qualified. It is such an elevated level of learning to qualify as a fitness professional.

At this point, I did not realise I was jumping out of the frying pan and into the fire. I did not yet realise that the pay was even worse than care work and I did not have sick and holiday pay. The last ten years have been one hell of a rollercoaster and not for the faint-hearted.

Do I regret leaving a fantastic paid job, good pension and being a homeowner? Not at all, as none of this would have meant anything if I could not see my son and ended up with a lifelong disability from too much stress and heavy lifting. I did miss London for a few years and took a while to settle into town life again after being a city girl.

I started to feel a bit poorly and despite going to the gym I was putting on weight. I was very trim after giving birth and I always stayed the same weight. I had some blood tests and it showed that I had an underactive thyroid brought on by the pregnancy. It was more due to all the stress before the pregnancy. I just thought I was tired from being a new mum.

Once I was on the right medication and better, I started to run classes at a local Martial Arts club and was part of an open day. I was offering free Reiki taster sessions to get to know the local community. Tom, who was on the Martial Arts team, had a Reiki session with me and then asked if I would be open to a new business opportunity. I said of course I am.

I was back in Network marketing again and the company is Utility Warehouse, which I have been a part of for the last eight years. I have had a bit of a break for the last couple of years and the reason I did so was something was missing, and I was not giving it my best.

I have fantastic people skills and networking skills, but my close rate was not adding up. I started to get the old patterns coming back. Not feeling good enough, comparing myself to others. Then why are others doing so well with this and I am not finding it easy? It was frustrating as I love the company and still do. The people within the company and the friends I have met along the way are still my friends and want me to come back.

I had an amazing time at the conferences and the incentives, and the rewards were five stars. It gave me a taste of the life that I wanted to work towards. I still use all the services and am still a big tech geek. I got asked many times why I decided on a Utility Warehouse and not a supplement or fitness company.

I loved the fact that I only had to sign up a customer once and they were already using the services. With products, you need to get repeat customers and must order stock. I wanted something that fit into my life. I had done products and you had to spend a lot each month and get a certain volume to get your commission. With this, I just needed to get to 50 customers to lock in my commission. It made total sense. Then lots of little providers came along at a much cheaper price and I lost loads of customers. I started to lose interest. I know it goes in waves but felt at an all-time low from working so hard and not seeing the results that I had expected.

This really bothered me as I am such a fantastic connector and networker. This is something that I do naturally. I was just in an area that was not seeing how good the services were. For me it was the timing and not having a car; It was very time consuming to do all the appointments on foot and my team also gave up. I was not giving my best as a leader. I knew I needed to come away for a while. I still had my customer base and with no team, I was not accountable to anyone so I was free to have that space to explore what was going on. The reason I joined was for personal development, and it took me on a different route for a while. I never expected such a brilliant turning point once I dug deep enough and found the right people to help me shift the last parts of the puzzle pieces.

Plus, I had a partner who did not support what I was doing. It is important that you are with someone who sees and supports you. It is better to be alone than have a relationship like that, so I stayed single for an exceedingly long time after that. The more my confidence grew, the more the relationship deteriorated. There is no point being with someone who is intimidated by success and puts you down to make them look good. So many stay in relationships just for the sake of being in one. I have never been like that and love being a free spirit, still wanting to be in a relationship and feel free.

I watched lovely couples within the network, and I got to see what it was like to have a partner fully supporting you and building you up. Not just the couples, but also the lovely people in the network wanting you to grow and be successful. The personal development side of the business was amazing, and I still utilise lots of what I learned into my business now and my writing and speaking career, which I am now steadily building up. It was great working for yourself having a massive team around you and routing for you to succeed. Having a community of like-minded people is what life is all about.

I did not quit and just parked this part of the business. As an entrepreneur, you have many different paths on your road to success. What I learned in these years was what has led me to author this book now. The stories I heard at the company events made me want to keep on getting better. I thought I would be going on the stage with UW, and who knows one day very shortly I may be going on in a vastly different capacity. I asked many times if I could speak and tell my story. I was told you are not ready. I found this very frustrating and worked so hard, but was not getting the results. It was so near yet so far.

Ellen Chant, who helped me a lot in the business, introduced me to Les Brown as a person to listen to. What an amazing motivational speaker. He was classed as dyslexic also and he had that hunger to succeed. I still listen to him regularly. His laugh is very infectious, and his tagline is "you gotta be hungry." It was great to be connected to lots of fantastic ambitious people who also wanted you to be successful.

One of my highlights in the company was qualifying for a space at Piggy fest which was a big party to celebrate half a million customers. It was an adult festival full of rides, camping, fireworks, live music, a free bar and loads of fun things to do. As a single mum, it was lovely to get away from it all and have some fun.

You will be glad to know that I am now back doing this business as I do very much enjoy it as I am helping people. I worked in social care doing the financial side as well as the health side for my clients. That was the beauty of the social care model. It looked at the person as a whole and not body parts.

When I do my money savings sessions, I go into it the same way as I would when helping people with wellness. When you are in debt, worrying about the bills has a massive impact on your wellbeing. Just living to pay the bills is not what life is about. Living in debt is even worse. It keeps you trapped into situations that you would have left years ago if you were not stuck in debt. I was in massive debt and did not see a way out. Just years and years or more of the same. This is not what I signed up for and therefore I speak up and tell others that there is another way. Not everyone is ready to hear this but at least you have given them a choice.

It was lovely to ease back into the business and it felt very natural. I did a lot of inner work so that I could enjoy what I was doing again. I had come with lots of baggage from years of working and being only called into the office when I had done something wrong. Being in network marketing is great as you get praised and rewarded for all the small steps along the way. You still get called out on your bullshit, but these lovely happy forward-thinking people want you to succeed, and that was the difference.

The pandemic also changed the business model as I struggled to build a team - now that more people have had a taste for working from home and not seeing it as just a hobby is tremendous. I had a lot of stick from people in the early years saying you will never make money in this. You need to get a proper job. It is the most grown-up proper job I have ever had. I feel ready to grow a team again and change lives. I am happy to say that I am back to what I love and helping people save money and make money. When you are worried about the bills it affects every part of your life.

More Month than Money

I had many years of juggling the bank account at 3 am and popping to the bank to pay a few quid in if an unexpected bill came out. Or someone did not pay me, and this left me short. I was so scared of asking people to pay me. I felt shame and embarrassment even though I was offering a service. I believe this unconscious belief of not being enough ran very deep. I am so glad I sorted this out and now ask for my worth. What is great about network marketing is the more you help others, the more you also help yourself. The old saying is you cannot pour from an empty cup or an empty bank account. It can make you very resentful.

I hated those lean years watching people able to buy what they want and not having to go shopping at the yellow sticker time. It was also hard to watch one of my clients in a supermarket saying I am just buying this salmon for my dog. I felt so fed up with this as people's pets were eating better than me. How can I promote health and wellbeing when I could not afford to eat well? Yes, I have been there big time. So, all of you who say to me, you are so successful, I could not do what you do. Think long and hard. If I can do it with no money, no car, not even wifi and also having dyslexia and dyspraxia on top... You can do it.

I have lots of patients and time for people who are willing to do the work. Therefore, I cannot work with people who are full of excuses and faff about. I want clear decisions, and then a whole heap of opportunities will fall on your lap. Yes, it will be hard, yes it will be a challenge, yes you will need to give up some deadenders or crap tv, yes you will give up weekends and evenings. Will it be worth it? - hell, yes? If you are prepared to do what others are not prepared to do for a few years to secure a better future for yourself and your family, then I am here for you all the way.

Do not wait until you have the money to get into a size 10 again. I just bought a bigger size. No, not skinny, as I have accepted my curvy figure. I just dress differently. We should not be expected to look the same way as we did in our 20s. It is a privilege to get older and I often wonder what those who have not liked themselves in their teens and 20s and went the surgical route will look like in later life. Looks like the outside package is just that. What we feel on the insides is what makes us shine brightly. A pretty face fades, but a kind face is what continues to shine.

We also must not beat ourselves up if we do not have a 7-figure income or any bricks and mortar assets. I have built mine up a few times and lost it all. I have watched many others who are entrepreneurs go the same route. If you have not sorted out the internal motherboard, then you will continue in a poverty mindset and sabotage any future success. Break that cycle today. It took me 50 years; you can start much earlier than I did. If I had been given a different opportunity at 18, then I would have taken it. Back in the 1990s it was all about exams and getting a job and then working until you retire and drop dead a few years later. Many did not retire. Live for today.

When Benjamin comes home from school saying, what is the point of school and sitting at a desk for 6-hours a day. I do all that work and do not get paid. He really struggles with maths and I had a look at the maths myself and my mum cannot understand it. I said you need to learn how to make money and learn how to do your accounts. I teach him the practical aspects. If he were able to start working for me today and give up school, he would. We struggled in lockdown as I did not see the point in what he was being taught and neither did he. Going through the school system was a waste of time for me and I find it extremely hard to hold my tongue when he comes home exhausted and feeling like he has failed. He said everything is done too fast.

I can relate to that. I needed to stop doing the exams against speed as they just put me in a panic. I can type at speed, but not read and answer questions at speed. Luckily, he is in an incredibly good school, and he is under Special Educational Needs.

He saw an Occupational Therapist recently and he did so well with balance, coordination and running. He was better than average. I have been training my son since he could walk. He still fell over most days until he was about 6 years old, but I was very persistent and kept him going. I got him a pull-up bar and he was training on my TRX Suspension trainer at age 5. I walked him everywhere and got him swimming from a few months old. He has dyspraxia also but no signs of the dyslexia side. He is an incredibly good reader but chooses not to. I think when he finds his passion, he will enjoy reading.

I wish I had this intervention when I was a child, but this was not the way back then. It was all about reading, writing and arithmetic. The last couple of years of school was much better as you could pick your subjects. I like sports but this was not an exam choice in the 1980s. I picked science and maths subjects. I wanted to become a nurse, but my grades at this point did not match what was needed. Thank goodness I kept going and took a different route. I was never a nurse in name but did everything that a nurse does. Maybe more than what the nurses do now as it is very much about exams and paperwork. Most of my training was on the job and not in a classroom.

Hands-on training is still the best way to learn.

Chapter 8

Living with the long-term effects of stress and burnout.

Baby brain and moving, plus all the stress of trying to finish my exams was a lot. Having dyslexia and dyspraxia on top was also an extra challenge. I was also feeling extremely tired, but despite this, I started to go back to the gym to stay in shape. My body snapped back in shape and I had a few people ask if I had just had a baby as I was in such good shape. Then my weight started to shoot up and had no idea why.

I eventually went to the GP, and they did tests, and it came back that I had an underactive thyroid. The GP was shocked at the reading and said it was a surprise that I was not on the floor as the normal reading is below 5 and mine was at over fifty. I was put on medication straight away. It took a long time to recover and ten years on I still need to be mindful of my energy.

I would try to still walk everywhere and keep up my fitness. I went to see a local lady about my back. She did acupressure and decided to book a session. She did checks and said you are not teaching yoga or Pilates yet, are you?

I said no. She said good as you need to have your full maternity leave to fully recover. I was still completing my Pre- and Post-natal modules so I was following this to the letter. That was such a beautiful part of my Fitness Diploma, I was able to be my own case study. I had filmed two DVDs whilst Pregnant. One was The Lazy Guide to Exercise and the Second one was Practical Pregnancy Pilates. I was planning to do Post Natal, but with the weight shooting up I did not feel ready to film that one. It was a long time before I got in front of the camera again.

As a single mum with little spare cash, I completed all my studies and ran the network marketing business. This was not the right product for this town though so gave that business up. I set up my fitness business from scratch in my hometown. I rebuilt my life and my reputation, but I wanted to regain my lifestyle back. Eating well, lovely walks, nice areas and having a car again. It took an exceptionally long time to rebuild my life again and had lots of big boulders in the road to overcome first.

Here is how it all started after my diagnosis.

For years I have studied nutrition and weight management. I first started getting interested in nutrition when I worked in a day centre for people with disabilities. Many of my clients had lots of weight issues that affected their day-to-day living. This often led to mobility problems, joint pain, diabetes, kidney disease, high blood pressure, and much more. Despite dieting and trying different methods, most failed to lose weight and would continue to gain. When you are in a wheelchair or struggle to move around then it makes things so much harder. As you get older, you start to lose muscle mass and your metabolism starts to slow down due to hormonal changes. So, you must eat and exercise differently.

My health issues are what led to me getting a greater understanding of the effects of diet and lifestyle and how it affects the emotions and the body and can lead to chronic conditions. If left untreated, this can lead to much more serious conditions. Therefore, I want to share the story of my struggles of living with a chronic illness.

I have never been on a diet in my life and always managed to keep my weight until I had my son. I have had digestive problems, bloating, and trouble with my blood sugar levels since having my son and I have had trouble shifting the weight. I have also had joint pains with chronic fatigue. I was diagnosed in 2012 with a post-pregnancy underactive thyroid, which then went on to full hyperthyroidism. I was put on thyroxine and was told to get on with it.

Despite being on the right dose, I was training five times a week doing a combination of weight, Pilates, yoga, suspension training, and up to two hours of walking every day. My weight stayed the same for four years and I still had a distended belly after eating healthy foods such as raw foods, onions, cauliflower, and types of meat.

I kept going to the doctors for more tests, such as vitamin D deficiency, more thyroid tests, liver function, kidney function, and more. All came back normal. I still did not feel right and had to have up to two naps a day to function. I am not sure how I did it; I was running two businesses, four classes plus private clients, and studying for my final exams. I had less than 300 pounds a month to spend on food, nappies, toiletries, and other essentials, which was not easy. I shopped locally, went to the market at closing time, shopping in the supermarket late at night, and was still short of money.

I had cheaper cuts of meat than I was used to and cooked with veggie mince as I am allergic to beef. I filled up with bread products and bought frozen fruit and veggies to make sure I never wasted any food. I also followed my friend's sugar-free recipes as she went through a similar journey to me concerning food intolerances.

When my fitness training and dietary changes were not working, I went back to the GP again. I even gave a food and activity diary to the doctor, and she just said you need to exercise more and eat less. I heard this time and time again with my clients and it is not as simple as that. I now know this firsthand and therefore I am telling my struggles.

My bloating started to get worse about September and continued to get worse up until May 2016. I even had to wear my baggy black yoga pants to teach in as I could not get into my usual exercise clothes. I felt tired, sluggish, fat, and very miserable. I went back to the doctor and still got no real help. I just kept getting told my thyroid levels were normal.

Then I met a lady called Emma who is a Medical Herbalist; I felt she could work with whatever medication I was on. I also study people's medication when I am planning exercise for my clients, so this was especially important for me to refer my clients to well-accredited professionals. I was meeting her about referring her to one of my clients but ended up referring to myself.

Before the meeting, I did a very extensive food and activity diary for two weeks. The first week I ate anything I fancied, to see what triggered my bloating and systems. The second week I ate what I would normally eat. This was a very emotional and eye-opening experience. I ask my clients to do this, but have never done a full one for myself. It is amazing how emotions are attached to food. The food I was eating was healthy; in fact, I was eating raw foods and salads with super greens, plus excellent quality supplements.

There are some companies that I like such as Forever Living and Arbonne as they have gone through rigorous testing, but you still need to consult with your doctor or dietitian to make sure they are ok for you. I am not a fan of fad diets as you could do more harm and then end up putting more weight on once you go back to normal eating. I prefer eating clean wholesome food. If I cannot read the ingredients, then I do not touch them. I am not a fan of low-fat diet food and use full-fat products instead-but less of it as it is more natural and not full of sugar.

I only recommend supplements to my clients that I know well and have been thoroughly assessed, as you need to know what you are doing, especially if you are working with medical conditions as it can affect people's medication. I had a full lifestyle analysis, which took about an hour and a half and then a medical examination. The aloe massage lotion was great on the joints though as I was getting shoulder problems and very stiff joints. I am very bendy, and the symptoms were hindering my ability to do my full stretches. Before the pregnancy, I could easily get my leg to my ear and into the full splits. I am there again now.

During the consultation, I was asked about past and present medical conditions - family history, stressful times in my life, and full diet and lifestyle questions; and then a series of tests such as BP, pulse, and looking at the tongue, and visual tests such as eyes, facial puffiness, and signs of inflammation.

The results of the medical tests were interesting. My blood pressure on the first visit was 120 over eighty-five, which is not a good result for someone so fit and my resting pulse was sixty. The figures did not make sense. This showed that something was wrong. All I got from the nurse was that I need to lose weight, and this will bring my blood pressure down. The blood pressure went up with the stress of seeing the nurse as they only go on BMI which does not consider fit people who have a high muscle mass and less body fat. I always measure my clients and test for body fat. Even though I weigh the same as I did four years ago, I was two dress sizes smaller. I responded very well with the treatment as I was willing to do the work. Just five weeks later I had lost three Kilos. My blood pressure went to what I would expect for my level of fitness - 110 over sixty and a resting heart of 65 bpm.

My body was just not functioning at an optimal level. No matter what healthy food, the exercise of supplements I was putting in my body, did not make any difference as my immune system and adrenals were not functioning properly. My body was intolerant to most raw food and salad, beans, onions, fish fingers, gluten, dairy and broccoli, and cauliflower. I was advised to cut my cardio workouts out and lift heavy weights instead.

Two months on, I still had bloating, but that was down to me still having the trigger foods, well I am human. I am still working on the chocolate and the bread. It is not a quick fix and a slow laborious process. Most people who have been on elimination diets say it takes a while for the mind to adjust to the changes. The biggest thing is my energy levels went through the roof, my stamina and endurance came back, and I am feeling extraordinarily strong. The puffiness went from my face, and I felt great. My goals are to keep working out what foods do not work for me, take aloe juice and herbal medicine.

So please, if you do not feel right and you cannot get a diagnosis from a medical professional, then you may benefit from trying a herbalist as they know how to work with chronic conditions and have more time to spend with you. Doctors and nurses are very pressed for time and may only have minutes to talk to you. Sometimes you need to take matters into your own hands and see what works for you.

Always tell your doctor first thought when embarking on an elimination diet or thinking of trying a treatment outside of the NHS. I found one doctor who was very understanding and was impressed that I was taking positive steps to get to the root of my illness. If my story helps just one person, then this will make me incredibly happy. I would love to hear from anyone who has had a similar experience.

Emma is now joining me and helping to support others who have similar issues and do not feel right despite following a healthy diet and keeping active. When I work with individuals, it is not about fad diets or quick fixes, it is about working with you as an individual to see what foods suit you and fit into your lifestyle. It is not about using complicated ingredients that are hard to find and that are expensive. It is about using local ingredients, organic if you can afford it, and food that most people have in their store cupboard or freezer. I managed it with little money, and I still had those weeks where there is more month than money, so I make big batches of food when I have the money and freeze the rest. So, in the leaner times, I can still eat well.

I was starting to feel much more like myself and started as a volunteer for the Council as a Health and Wellbeing Champion. It was only a couple of days a week and was a way to find out about the local community. I really enjoyed it, and this led me to re-starting my fitness business. I got a class at the local leisure centre teaching Pilates, and I started to run a class at the local Martial Arts Centre teaching Pilates and Yin Yang. I had a steady flow of clients. Not enough to earn a proper wage, but it was a start.

Chapter 9

Yoga Teacher Training

I wanted to keep Yoga special for me, so I did not train as a yoga teacher until 2018. This preparation was one of the hardest endeavours I have ever done. I had to take the dreaded anatomy exam again - 100 hours of anatomy. I had already earned an A level in anatomy and physiology, but it was a struggle from start to finish.

It was not in a learning style that I could process. I was not able to do any reasonable adjustments as it was online, and the course was set up to be done the way it was done. I did get through it eventually but missed finishing the 500 hours. I was disappointed but wanted to get out there and teach Yoga, but my way. I just wanted the certificate and had no real attachment to the yoga school. I had done my in-person training in London, and this was only a means to an end. You must do what you must do sometimes to get to the bigger vision. It was not the way I envisaged doing my yoga teacher training.

I imagined going on a two-month intensive on a beautiful tropical island but being a single mum, this was the best option for me.

I was used to filming and teaching online, so it was a shock that it took me about 200 attempts to pass the sun salutation video, which was about three minutes long. I had guns of steel by the end of filming. I was just one breath out of each video and would they let it go. Nope, it had to be concise Vinyasa. Do I teach like that now? No is the short answer.

I asked for an extension and a break before I went onto the 300 hours section of the course. I had studied all of it, but my brain felt like it had been twisted inside out and rung out. Not the way I wanted to feel during the course. The contents were fantastic, but I just could not do it in the period. It was a 12-month cut-off. I think they could have had leeway. This was not meant to be a totally unique experience from Future Fit and the Open University who were a fantastic support. All courses need to be client-led and not just about ticking boxes.

It was a shame as the 300 section was all about the energetics of the body. I enjoyed this more than the 200 hours which mainly contained the 100 hours of Anatomy, which I hated having to do again and did ask if I could cross-reference what I had already done twice. This is so wrong having to do it again and I had forgotten what I had to learn. It was just a pointless exercise. Yet again having to fit the mould to pass a stupid exam so that I am covered. It makes me angry when I see people who are not qualified that teach. I had lots of places putting me down as a yoga teacher and I kept pointing out that I am not qualified in yoga. Yes, I was practising for decades but having that certificate is key. I have most definitely got the qualifications and the bloody t-shirt. Once I got the paper I went back to my natural style. This was not my method of learning. I did what I had to do and did as I was told. It was a means to an end. I got a very unexpected gift from it. My love of making videos and teaching online.

I have a real passion now for teaching online yoga. I did do a class in person but found I love teaching online. I still also love being a yoga student. I got asked to teach a couple of classes at a yoga studio, but I felt the burnout symptoms coming back so decided I wanted to do more online teaching. Teaching more classes was no longer for me. I wanted to leverage my time and reach more people. I still need to be incredibly careful with my energy and make sure I am not working too hard.

I find that doing no more than seven classes a week is enough for me. I was getting offers to teach more classes, but this was too much for me. Especially being a single mum, trying to also run the household and the rest of the businesses. Studying took its toll on me and I needed recovery time. I gave up teaching yoga for a while to just go back to enjoying yoga just for me.

How the Stretch Zone was born.

I have been running Facebook groups for years and had a YouTube channel set up from just before my son was born. I had wanted to set up an online business for an exceptionally long time and now was the right time. Jane Scanlan was a lady and a friend that I had followed and watched online for an exceptionally long time. She had a business model that I wanted to run as an online holistic business. Jane was running an exclusive offer, so I joined her on a free trial and booked onto a three-month coaching program. From this, The Stretch Zone was born.

Jane has neurodivergent conditions herself, so she could relate to the obstacles that I came across and her coaching was everything that I was looking for. Not rushed and you have lifetime access to the content of all the courses that you purchase. She is deeply knowledgeable and really knows her stuff.

My problem was that I have so many skills; Jane was able to get me to focus on one thing at a time and decided to take the nutrition side of my business out of the equation for the time being. I was able to truly decide and concentrate on the online teaching side. I am not an early riser yogi and come alive at night so teaching later in the event suited me. I was not able to teach late at studios but teaching from home was perfect. My son was at home safe and near the fridge, if he needed snacks. No petrol costs and hall costs. I was also better off timewise. It would often be a long round trip to take my son to a childminder and the travel time. One hour's teaching took three hours of my time. This was also a situation that my clients would face so the idea of The Stretch Zone was born.

A safe space to offer my services for clients who wanted to learn yoga and spirituality in the comfort of their own home. I noticed that people wanted evening classes but were not able to get out due to caring roles, childcare, travel issues, or anxiety disorders. For me, yoga was never about looking good. It was what kept me sane, and I wanted to help run my services in a way that would reflect this side.

I do extraordinarily little yoga, but I do yoga. Let me repeat that. I do truly little of the yoga that you think is yoga, but when I am teaching yoga people do not think it is yoga. It was like when I had Pilates as part of my Diploma. I said I did not want to learn Pilates as I am a yogi. It was only when I started learning Pilates that I realised I had been doing it for years in Yin Yang and did not know. So, we do not really know what we are learning, and we are just going along with it. If you are enjoying what you are doing and getting the desired results, then that is the main thing.

I still follow the Iyengar yoga system to this day even though this is not the discipline in which I have trained. I did spend over 10,000 hours doing Iyengar practice and this is worth so much more than the 200 hours of yoga teacher training. Well, 500 hours but I did not complete that as I felt rushed, and they did not understand my neurodiversity needs. Any course that I run will and does cater for all levels of neurodiversity and neurotypical. I want to be that person who will have students saying I really felt heard and that my needs were met and that was a very enjoyable experience.

None of the courses that I did were a pleasant experience when it came to the exam process apart from Reiki. This is the area I excelled in as it was Kinesthetic learning. This is also why I teach Iyengar as I was there feeling the feelings. Online is great for many things but being fully present and being in the room is priceless. I will not be one of those Reiki Master or Yoga Teachers that will teach the full course online. I will only ever attune my Reiki students in person and will continue with this legacy. The way my masters taught me. Direct practical hands-on learning.

The online community that I have created are all people that I have mainly met in person, and this will be a legacy that I will continue to push. Virtual coffee chats and retreats will never be the same as in the flesh meetups. Just like when I advocated for my clients to keep being able to go to the shops as opposed to the cheaper option of having food delivered as part of their care package. We are social animals and need social interaction. We need to feel valued and have a sense of self - to self-actualize and grow to be the best we can be.

Online has its place and now my classes can go global as opposed to local. People mainly join the group if they have anxiety, confidence issues, who are not ready to go to a gym or they can feel intimidated in mainstream classes. Many start to go to actual classes and continue with the online to complement the in-person classes.

Overthinking and not being able to sleep is also one of the reasons people join. I had one lady do my classes at 3 am as she was not able to sleep. The Stretch Zone is not for everyone as it is slow, gentle, and relaxing. Some people love fast, energetic, and masculine. I can be all of these in my Boxolates and in-person classes. Many thought it was going to be all of these things. I did try, but without the music blasting from an amazing sound system this was not the same.

I had to buy special music to teach online. I hated teaching on Zoom and the music sounded distorted from all the different bandwidths filtering the music through. I am such a perfectionist when it comes to teaching online, so it was best to have no music for Zoom. I prefer livestream or videos. Lots of teachers love to use Zoom but this is not for me. I do teach on Zoom and have coaching on Zoom. I get Zoom fatigue; Zoom was not created for teaching Yoga. So, I teach to my best with The Stretch Zone material.

Chapter 10

Visionary future aided by Visionary leaders

What a legend. Louise Hay was ahead of her time and when I listen to her, she makes total sense. She was very much part of what is called the LGBTQIA+ movement before it became as big as it has. She set up meetings for young gay men to help them feel good about themselves and build up their self-worth and self-esteem. She worked with them on a very deep level. This was back in the early 1990s with an unconscious bias towards sexism, racism and discrimination were horrendous. We still have a way to go, but credit where credit's due, she was a true pioneer. If you are into personal development, then this is a lady to read about. Her full audiobook is on YouTube. I still listen to her book when I need to get back on track myself.

I want people with the neurodiversity movement to become as big as the LGBTQIA+ movement and make the changes necessary so that people are treated as individuals as opposed to being judged on sexuality or the ability to pass exams. We have lots of people who are lost in the system due to not being able to keep up with the system as it is. The Apple Complex is a company that fully embraces the unique minds of neurodiverse people. If you had people who can pass exams easily in the normal way, then they would struggle to thrive in the Apple environment.

What I have found interesting is you are drawn to the right teachers. The saying goes when you are ready your teacher arrives. Earlier in my Reiki chapter, I mentioned Wanya and Phyllis. Two of my masters are writers also, and Wanya (who taught Louisa) was also a fantastic storyteller and writer. I was fascinated by her storytelling. She had the most mesmerising, engaging cheeky bright blue eyes. I heard stories straight from Wanja herself of her running Reiki shares in Canada. I have been to Reiki shares in total silence, but Wanja had a real presence and community feel to her Reiki shares. Laughter, food, and lots of storytelling. This has filtered down to my teaching. Louisa introduced me to Reiki shares, and I was hooked. The gathering which Wanya attended was the turning point for me. I was very drawn to her energy. I met Phyllis a couple of years later and was drawn less to her energy but had a massive amount of gratitude and respect for her.

Phyllis was more inward and thoughtful. You would ask her a question and she would go deeply within and then give you an answer that you needed to hear and not necessarily what you thought you wanted to hear. She looked beyond the question and investigated the energy behind it. I saw Phyllis truly blossom over the next few years and felt totally blessed that I had the opportunity to meet her and even sit at the same table as her. She looked so happy in her final years. I felt so privileged that I got to learn through Wanja and her lineage and learned the different feel of the energy with Phyllis and her lineage. To anyone who is not familiar with Reiki, this is your Reiki Timeline, like a family tree that you can trace back. This is particularly important as you cannot be accredited or insured without this. Learning Reiki from a book would not have been the same for me. I got to meet everyone firsthand and experience the energy in person. Reiki was very traditional when I joined but it has now moved online, especially in the last few years. Phyllis was amazing at doing question and answer webinars in her final years. Plus, Reiki shares via Zoom happened during the lockdown. The whole Reiki community started to come together again.

We are the silent army. We were all doing our bit on an energetic level to keep the vibration high in a particularly challenging time. We were supporting each other so that we were able to support the community. The lightworkers and the earth angels were coming out from all corners of the world. It was a challenging time for the masses. Many of us are used to being very insular and working in the energetic world, we did not feel as affected. I am not going too deeply into this in this book as quantum physics is a book. The power of the mind is so vast, and we are still learning about this on a scientific basis.

Hence my fascination with Dr. DeMartini who is incredibly famous for his motivational speaking and an author of hundreds of books. He has dyslexia and he inspired me to want to create my own legacy. He led me deeper into the personal development world which led me to become a leader.

The Digital age for me was like a breath of fresh air. I learned to touch-type, and then I can type as fast as my thoughts come into my head. Copying from a chalkboard was too time-consuming for me. My brain worked too fast and then forgot what I was copying. I type as fast as possible, and my brain dumps my thoughts. It is then tidied up later. Getting the thoughts down is more important than worrying about what I call the faffy bits. Those who love the faffy bits can do those bits for me. Although I can spot a mistake very quickly. I like to see writing perfectly polished. When given the right equipment, anyone can become a writer and get the thoughts down in a tangible way that everyone can understand. Writing is like art; we are all drawn to unique styles of writing.

Transformation

When I started to author my transformational book, this led me on a very unexpected journey. In the global pandemic, I have grown so much more than I have ever done in almost 50 years.

I have done things far beyond what I ever expected to achieve, and this is not in the so-called academic achievement but on a deep soul level. This is an incredibly special year as I am coming up to my 20th anniversary of becoming initiated into Reiki. Like many people, I became lost in lockdown. The things that you take for granted to cope with and when taken away you realise how utterly vulnerable you are and how special friends and family are. You must dig deep and show who you are and not hide behind a smokescreen.

I realised that I could not carry on the same way as I did before lockdown. Lockdown was about being alone and living in a quite unusual way. I am a very solitary person naturally so I really embraced this time to dig deep and look at ways I can truly show up and be of a true purpose and service. I spoke in-depth during my first chapter in Wild Women Rising about being told repeatedly that I am not for purpose. I want to inspire whoever reads this book that no matter how your life began or how your family believes that this is the way - you can be the one to change history. We carry on so many stories and how family and history shaped your life. You have control of your destiny.

What has been the biggest breakthrough has been serving others and being of service to others with my incredibly unique gifts. Ones that have been taken for granted that others know how to do, just as those who tried to teach me a schooling system that did not work for me and many others before me. Leading to a chain of ancestors who did not know and were different and passed this on to the new lineage. Victims of Victims. We do not know what we do not know.

I have tried many different modalities to try to fix the family tree for past and present timelines. Having done lots to heal me, I still felt I did not have to the root or the core of what was going on. I felt like I had an incredibly old 486 computer program, which was one of the very first computers back in the 1990s that was accessible in people's homes. It seems like yesterday but a very essential aspect of history. I dated a highly intelligent guy back in my 20s and he was very ahead of his time, gifted but very flawed, but only in society's eyes at that time.

So back to the computer. I felt like every day when I woke up, I had to reboot and go through all the old programming systems. It was a slow and exhausting, long boring wait to fully reboot. It was like wading through malaises. Even with all the healthy stuff I do, and I do wake up massively grateful, I felt that there must be an easier way of waking up. I had seen my ex-fiancé take apart computers, put them back together, and reprogram them to a better fully functioning version. One that boots up in a generated, invigorated, and highly functional model. The mother of all processing systems.

Since becoming a bestselling author in lockdown, I began to see what a gift I had and how my struggles against adversity, prejudice, and growing up in the 1970s and 1980s helped me to pave the way for future generations and share what I have learned along the way.

Without the long twisting winding road back to self who was never broken in the first place but was led to believe they were because you were made to conform and fit inside and box. It is my life mission to show you how to unleash yourself from this so-called box and get so far out of the box that you invent the bloody box. I have spent far too long being on the outside looking in and showing that you do not need to be in a box. When working for social services, there were so many different boxes to tick.

When my son started school, I was asked what religion he is. I said I have no idea; I will let him decide that. I wanted to initiate him into Reiki, but even at just 6, he said I will let you know when I am ready if ever. I learn so much from the younger generation and the older generation. Community is the heart of everything that I ever do. I did not come from a family of wealth but what we lacked in so-called consumerism wealth we had in values and integrity. Strong community and family values.

The beauty I have seen in this pandemic has been mind-blowing. The local and worldwide connections have been mesmerising. The beautiful souls that I connected with on my travels and London have been life-changing. We have not met in the in-person form but connected on a much deeper emotional level. Showing up as raw, unfiltered, and vulnerable. Truly being able to slow down and truly be. Truly be present. I have been practising yoga for almost four decades and it is only now that I truly got to that true peace of mind and enlightenment.

Having this time, I realised how much I have been doing and not having the time to reflect and enjoy the glory of the achievements. I never thought I would be live streaming to a page with 23,000 followers teaching Yin Yang, when I said yes, I thought it was to a group of about 200.

I never expected to become a bestselling author in lockdown and get so confident in front of the camera I do not care if it is one person or a million. I went live in lockdown with lockdown hair. Those who live in this area know that is important when we live in a society that rewards the way we look and celebrity culture. When I learned yoga, we had bloomer pants and vests. No selfies, no Instagram, no filters. It was a place to just be and to just feel. No looking in the mirror, no man or woman. We all had to look the same and nobody looks good in yoga bloomers. I have no picture of those and would not be sticking them on Instagram.

Anyone who joins my yoga classes will get my practice, not out of a book, not by following YouTube but with lifelong dedication. We had to go into the feeling. Living in London was hard to feel as it was a doing place. Yoga and Reiki are what gave me sanctuary in the chaos. Sorting out the internal motherboard.

Through my lovely book coach, I met a fantastic lady called Dounia. Even though I had achieved so much success in my life, something was wrong with me and I could not achieve what others do even though I have done more than many do in a lifetime. I was fast approaching 50 and wanted to be able to enjoy the next half a century and share my passion and gifts. Leave a legacy for myself and future generations.

I had this old program going on and on and doing my head in. The noise was getting louder for me to sort it out. I had created many transformations for my clients and was getting frustrated that I could not tap into this block I had. The perfectionism, the people-pleasing, beating myself up, and not fully being present. I have often been in a state of anxiety and rumination. Catastrophizing things in my head rather than just going with the flow. This stemmed from seeing things as too hard and not even getting started. This was when I decided enough is enough and invested in me. Not a fancy holiday, clothes, or stuff. I needed to sort my internal motherboard out. Going back to Mother Nature and coming back pure and whole and fully back to self.

Money had been tight in the pandemic, and I tried every angle to get funding. I hit many roadblocks and refused to conform just so I could fit into a box to get funding. I stuck to my guns and stayed true to myself. I am ahead of my time with knowing when to take a real risk that will benefit the highest of good for all. I cannot serve others from a victim or poverty mindset. So, I stuck it on my credit card. I took that leap of face to get that quantum leap. The universe rewards those who take massive action and do not stay stuck with the internal so-called norm.

The old values were holding me back. Being alone for most of the pandemic with only myself and my son meant that I must take a long hard look at myself. I do not lay my soul bare to anyone and I immediately was drawn to Dounia. She had a mix of Real Beauty inside and out and an incredibly unique quality about her. She had the ability to see into your soul, to draw out what is already there, a pure safe channel to tap into your true potential with ease and grace. I had no nasty comedown, no nasty flashbacks, just an easy, peaceful, and graceful healing process. There were no withdrawals and no going into painful past experiences. You get to re-write your own exceptionally beautiful book on your terms and conditions.

After the very first session, I felt different. I felt very hungry for the first week. I have lived for years with IBS and digestive issues and I felt so much better and had a normal appetite for the first time in years. I was also getting full very quickly. I no longer had to squash down the emotions and the stuff of generations before. After the second session, I felt like I had been on holiday. I felt so vibrant and fully able to feel and see. I was hearing music in its full entirety and feeling my body. I slowed down the yoga and fully got back into classes for me. When posting now on my platforms I think to myself how this comes across as Dounia is watching aka Big Brother. Sandra and I have this nickname for her. We all want to show our true beautiful authentic selves. She is like the mother hen of our tribe.

Many people kept putting my classes down as Yin Yang yoga. The Yin Yang I learned was martial arts. Working with the qi helps me to tap into the Reiki and the higher self. You will not get this level of my practice and only in my private memberships as it is an incredibly special and deep practice. One that comes with lifelong learning and dedication. I have not learned what I have learned from a book but in the full embodiment of being in the process on the long winding twisting road to self-acceptance.

The holiday feeling is still with me. I still have bumps in the road, they are now few and far between. I was so used to the old feeling, reactions, and emotions that it took me a while to get used to the new me. For example, going from being twenty stone to ten stone. Or from not having money to winning the lottery.

Authoring the book over the last 12 months has been an incredibly busy time, but a good one. A busy place where I was not chasing people and chasing my tail. Opportunities have been coming to me with ease and grace. My dream of becoming a motivational international speaker is now happening. I have been a guest expert speaker on the BBC talking about how I changed my business in lockdown and transformed it. I have been invited to speak at The Dyslexia Association in London via Zoom talking about Neurodiversity and how getting a diagnosis changed my life. Most recently, I went stateside and got interviewed by Zachary, who is a four times Best Selling International Author, talking about The Law of Attraction. Plus, enjoying the fabulous coffee morning chats with Sandra, my book midwife and friend.

I have had Facebook try to shut me down a few times for speaking my truth about my values and beliefs and created a funny photo of myself looking like Ali G saying, You can shut me down, but you cannot shut me up. I have a message to deliver, and it is an important message. Many people have said to me that I could never write a book. I would say to those just watch me. If I can author a book as a single mum with writing as my least easy ability as well as being told that I was lazy at school and would not amount to anything, then get on with it. You do not know what is around the corner.

I now run my business the way I have always wanted to run it. When I first started, heartfelt businesses were not the norm and were seen as hobby businesses. It was all about big corporate and product-based. Now people are very much the heart of the business and the face behind the business. When I am promoting my business, I am doing it in a few different formats. I do a written newsletter weekly to show a list of things that are happening for the week. This is mainly copied and pasted and just tweaked to the new week. I have lots of time-saving times and anyone who gets to work with me will get three decades of business and time-saving hacks. I do not faff and fuss so anything that makes my life easier and others, I will look for that route.

I do a video of the week's offerings and events for those that like to hear and watch what you have to say. For me, my favourite learning style is auditory and sensory. I do many of my videos with just me speaking and doing a guided meditation of yoga class so that you can connect to your senses. This is called kinesthetic learning and it is a tactile learning style that uses movement, testing, trial and error and a nontraditional learning environment to recall and retain information.

I use oils and music, dance, and meditation to help recall information and to get my messages out there. When I was trying to do exams, I would take my oils in with me so that I could associate the smell with the recall in my mind. Singing and dancing certain parts would enable me to tap into that section of my brain to recall. When session planning for my classes, I go for a swim and a sauna first and then decide on the mix of music I am going to use then the session plan is done. I have spent years drawing stick people for my session plans for yoga and Pilates and would stick different hairstyles on them from all diverse cultures. I wanted to make them stand out and come alive.

Music, arts, and culture is my passion, and this shows through in my workshops and classes. I do not stick to the rule book. I create my own rule book and am finally ready to teach my own method to the world. The Kelly Method is full of kellyisms which one day could become a new language. Who says the English Language is the right way? It is now full of many antiquated words that now need to be modernised and replaced with unfamiliar words that reflect the new world.

Somebody needs to be the innovator and the visionary to make the necessary changes to pave the way for the next generation. I am going to be 50 when this reaches you and this is my generation's time to step up and make the changes. You hear a lot about the baby boomers and the millennials, but you do not hear much about Generation X which is my generation. We were the first generation to be told you can have it all and it has not been the case at all. Many from this generation are often a bit lost. We came through the Thatcher years and austerity. There were not many job opportunities and University was only for the elite.

I remember watching Educating Rita, a movie about a hairdresser from a working-class northern background going to university. She got stuck from both sides - from the posh university types and from the people in her town. The more she became educated, the more she was seen as a threat. We get used to you being a certain way and acting a certain way. University changed me and gave me choices. I did not want to be stuck on a care assistant's wage forever. Less than a tenner an hour for doing one of the hardest jobs in the world. I want to be an advocate and speak from the outside as when you are on the inside you are told to put up and shut up and told this is how it is. It does not have to be this way.

Stop paying footballers extortionate money for kicking a ball about and give those with real balls and drive a proper wage, decent health care to keep them maintained with regular health checks and physio. Why should carers end up with chronic health issues and end up on the scrap heap for looking after their loved ones? Then have nobody to look after them when they are no longer fit for purpose. People before profit and then we will see a change in the system.

I see such waste in the councils and it is not about throwing money at an already haemorrhaging system.

Bring back the community and put the money back into social care and this overall will help save the NHS. Nobody wanted to listen to us who knew the system inside out. The people I most respected in my job were the Administrators, the caretakers, and the domestics. If one of them went off sick, then the entire day was much harder. If a suit was off, it did not make a blind bit of difference. They just made the job harder by piling on more red tape and paperwork. Clipboard managers, I called them. Walking around with a clipboard to try to make them look important.

I started as a care assistant because the school career adviser did not know what to do with me so they said they would stick me in a care home. My Grandad was immensely proud as he knew how well I looked after my Nanna. He said not everyone can do what you do, and it takes an incredibly special person to do that job. It was seen as a very demeaning low paid job. One day my big vision is to see this flipped on its head and suits get paid an admin wage and care workers get paid a specialist wage. Now that is something I want to see in my lifetime, and I am going to do my bit to make sure that happens.

My Why is bigger than me.

Stories are what beautifully bring businesses to life. Gone is the world of spreadsheets and people having meetings about which meeting to have - the clipboard experts. You cannot pretend you are doing well; I was brought up in the wave of the fake it until you make it culture. I never felt comfortable with the borrowed belief and wanted to be my unique authentic self.

It has been like coming full circle and coming back to self - the long twisting winding roads to acceptance. We are whole and complete just the way we are, perfectly imperfect.

The last couple of years has been more about connecting to energy. The Yin and the Yang, the masculine and feminine energies, Quantum leaps and Quantum Physics, the Chi or Prana, the ebb and flow of life, going with the flow of nature and the natural cycle of life. For many years we have been following a system that does not work for the masses. We are all unique and have our natural way of perceiving the world.

This has been a period of rest and reflection. A time to just be and enjoy the beautiful blessings in life and be truly present.

I have also become less of a people pleaser and less tolerant of listening to other people's drama. Years later you hear people going on about the same old shit. The ones who only ever go on about themselves and do not notice that you have moved on. They know nothing about your life.

The pandemic was a weird time and I felt like a hologram at times. I had created my online business long before COVID hit and people thought that because I was teaching yoga and Pilates online, I wanted to teach everyone. I have been working on my niche for decades and that has not deviated at all. I look after adult children, and I mean that in the nicest possible way. People who are full of adventure and want to live life to the fullest and nothing stops them from living their best life.

Not the ones who think they are entitled and want a free ride. I had a lot of people join me in lockdown and then when I asked for payment they were horrified and said that everyone is doing it for free on the internet. I replied I am not Joe Wicks, and he is more than welcome to teach you little darlings, but he is not doing it for free and will come out of this an even richer man. So again, we come down to this - why do people pay so little regard to their health and not think they need to pay for it. People treat their cars better than they do their health and when it packs up and they get ill then they blame everyone and everything for it.

I did my absolute best to keep the more vulnerable people moving in lockdown and had lots of lovely loyal people who do value their health and value my expertise. Those that did not were quickly eradicated. They can go off and get all the free stuff. My knowledge is decades of study against the medical and social model of health and social welfare. Not some influencer who looks good and gets to be the voice of some all fur and no knickers campaign with no real substance. I felt like a hologram during my Facebook lives whilst teaching and people did not realise that I was a real live person teaching these sessions.

Repeatedly the government said we were not essential, and they kept the fast-food restaurants open and then had a go at us for getting fatter. It is like sticking a plaster over a festering wound. It will come back to fully bite us all on the bottom. I saw the obesity crisis happening 30 years ago and gave lots of advice on measures that we could take to prevent this from happening - the use of the car and the big supermarkets, as well as the loss of the high street, has been the major impact on how we now live. The high street was the hub of the community.

Something that stuck in my mind was education. I cannot remember what this study was about, but the birth control pill was given to a community in Africa to prevent unwanted pregnancy without any education and advice on how to use it. They planted the pills. What is this got to do with now you may ask.

I have seen over the years a massive decline in the social care model and all the money going into the NHS. It used to be a lot more balanced and the money that went into social care services cut down the need for people needing the NHS. Now we may be living longer but we are living a lot longer in poor health and long-term chronic conditions.

One big example was the closing down of many sure start children's centres. These were the education centres for the poorest in our communities teaching young parents how to cook and basic accounting and courses to help people get an education and find a pathway out of the benefits system. Young parents no longer have this guidance and with the loss of the high street and local jobs, there is also a loss of childcare from having to move away to earn a living. So, all the money goes to childcare.

Multi-generational homes were the norm just half a century ago. No support and guidance from the older generation and trapped in the benefits system. The older generation are often living alone, and the loss of older services are closing leading to more illness and isolation. The lockdown has yet to see the wider cracks that are there, but many could not see until now when it is affecting everyone. It has become essential that we take full autonomy over our own lives. In a way, the NHS and the benefits system has left many of us in learned helplessness of living within the system and I will get looked after if anything happens.

It is best to start paying attention now and make sure that you put your health at the top of your list, not the fancy car or the fancy house. Put the best food you can afford into your body. Give it a good run around or a dance around the living room. Do something meaningful and look at how you can be of service to others. Once you look outside of yourself and see the full bigger picture then you can have influence.

Many people just sit back and wait for stuff to just happen around them. Be initiative-taking and not reactive. We only get one crack at this so leave a legacy for the future generation. As Generation X it is my generation that is leading the way for the next few generations. We are the sandwich generation who are fighting for the rights of the older generation whilst leading the way for the younger generations while being guided and listening to what is being said on both sides.

I will give you an example of this. Tonight, I was triggered, yes proper triggered and yes this is not proper grammar English this is the way I speak and the language a lot of my local community speak. I put a post out on Facebook, and someone pulled me up on my grammar. It would be more influential if your bloody English were even basic. What!!!!!! Who gives a flying fig. I said I have Grammarly to sort out that grammar shit and that I am a bestselling author. If you get your point across then who cares about the grammar. I speak in a user-friendly language and not pretentious crap that has been taught for years to make people look better than they really are. Does being able to write well make you a better person? So, what if someone gets their "to" "too" "two" crap wrong, who made up this stupid language in the first place. I see recently that the American spelling is going to become more mainstream. This makes more sense to me as the American spellings are spelt more like you speak and not in some portentous way. Spell it as you speak. It is a no brainer.

I had this at work one day. I was doing a presentation and had some bright spark saying you spelt that wrong. I looked her directly in the eye and said listen to what I have to say and not what is on the whiteboard. She soon shut her mouth up. I do not mince my words when it comes to this kind of judgement.

Conclusion

Becoming unfiltered again

Have I always been this unfiltered, yes even more so when I was younger. I had to curb it and become more of a so-called lady-like. I did not see myself any different from the boys, so could never understand why I was not allowed to fight and swear just like the boys who get angry. This just festered inside for years and would just explode into emotional eruptions. Calm for a long time and then just erupt like a volcano. They call these meltdowns now. My emotions needed to come out. Many of us had that pressure cooking going on growing up. Some of the things that were said to us: You have nothing to be stressed about; You are too young to have any worries; Girls do not swear and start fights. I did not see why I was different because I was born a girl. I wanted to have the same opportunities as the boys.

Even now in 2021, girls are only just being diagnosed with autism and Asperger's. Boys outwardly display what was going on, but with the "shut up you are a girl" thing going on, we went inwards and internalised emotions.

Then we got you to be too emotional, or too sensitive. Then the acting begins. This is now called masking. I studied people long and hard and just copied what they did as I had no clue how I was meant to do things as the way I did things I was being told that it was wrong, so I was acting to fit in.

I lost myself for a while after becoming a mum and no longer having a salary and a regular stream of income. The fitness industry is even worse than social care for paying people their worth. I get no sick and holiday pay and if classes go low when people do not turn up then I still have the same bills to pay. It was a hard decade of building up a business in my hometown.

I did lose sight of my goal for a while and became stuck in the benefits system myself. I am only just getting out of the benefits trap now and lockdown during the global pandemic was a blessing in many ways. I was used to not having money to go out. It has been a massive learning curve being in the benefits cycle. This gave me a great awareness of the community coming from personal experience and obtaining a chronic illness myself. Becoming fully immersive and engaging in different people's shoes allowed me to become fully empathic.

I have been very judgmental of people, and it is not until you fully work in those shoes that you will fully understand. I am also a lot more tolerant of people. I had on the surface patience and understanding of people but needed lots of time away from people. I enjoy time on my own. I had a boss say to me you spend a lot of time in your head. I thought that was a very weird thing to say and thought where else I am supposed to be. For me, everything is in your head. I do get what she was on about and she meant I should be more on this planet and not in my head fantasising and wishing I were anywhere else but my job at the time.

As an introverted extrovert, I need reflection time. I need to have that time to work things out in my head before I can move my physical body. I have this planner in my head working it all out first. I work out how long I need to get up and get everything ready. I run a vast number of different options in my head of what is the best plan of action. Lots of coaches teach these methods to their students when getting ready for races and training events. The mind is an immensely powerful thing. We only use a tiny amount of its capacity. It is the same with phones and computers.

We only use a small percentage. There is no need to keep updating your phones every year. We need to utilise what we already have and expand on that. We overcomplicate things. I still used pen and paper for my planning. Even authoring this book has had its challenges. I am using Word and it keeps signing me out, so I emailed it to several people to make sure I never lost anything. If you have no hard copies or backup, then you have lost it. Having paper copies makes things seem more real. I do not appreciate electronic books as much as I do an actual physical book. I do not read in the traditional way. I often flick through a book, especially personal development books and reference books. It is a bit harder to do that online.

We live in a world that overcomplicates things to show self-importance that is not necessary. What we all need is to feel heard and connected. Nobody really cares how much you own but how you make people feel. I have tried to simplify lots of courses over the years in the delivery so that they are in a more user-friendly way to everyone and not just to the ones that are easily able to learn in the so-called traditional way which is not that traditional. Back in history, communication was nonverbal and explained in picture form. People expressed themselves with creativity, music, and dance. Medicine was a mixture of healing, prayer, herbs, and nature.

I wanted to author this book to show that you can do anything that you put your mind to. This whole structure that we have known does not serve a vast amount of the population. We are told to do endless hours of mindless structured lessons at school which does not work now in society. It did not work when I was at school, and my son comes home feeling the same way as I did. Asking me what the point of this subject and algebra is. He is very much like me, wanting to know the point of certain subjects before spending years of your life doing it to never have to use it again. He says on a weekly basis how many more years of this do I have. Why does the weekend go so fast and why is there not another way?

I am his mother, but see his point in its entirety. I went to an open evening at his school in preparation for his exams. They were doing all the working out on paper. I said, is it necessary as we all have phones now so we will just work it out on the phone. Back in the 1970s, we were told we would not always have a calculator on us. We now have a full office in our pocket. We need to get with the program and not keep teaching a system that does not work for many. We then get a job, work till we retire and move to a small room with just a few memories and extraordinarily little items.

We just have so much unnecessary stuff. Then we feel anxious, cluttered, and overwhelmed. I have met many millionaires in my time, and they still feel the same way.

What we need is connection, acceptance, and the freedom to be. We have lost that community connection and live very insular lives full of likes and follows which mean little. If the electricity went out tomorrow, to whom would you turn? I have lived most of my life being of service to others and we need connection and human contact to be truly content. Not happy as that is not a realistic expectation. We do not need to be happy all the time. We need to embrace all aspects of our souls.

At the beginning of this book, I started with the question.

Who am I?

I end with something for you to think about.

This is a real case scenario and there is no right or wrong answer.

Giving the choice of having a fully functioning mind or a so-called perfect size ten body.

Which would you choose?

I have a few fascinating stories on this very subject and if you want to know my answer to this and you have a curious mind then I would love to hear from you.

Raw and unfiltered
Let the journey begin.

AFTERWORD BY JANE SCANLAN

Kelly and I connected through mutual holistic friends and hit it off instantly at a hippy wellness weekend festival! We had so many similarities, both single parents since pregnancy, both kids the same age, both the odd one of the family, both wellness business owners, both neurodiverse, both wanting more out of life and both secret super stars!

Why Secret? Well, we were both hiding behind masks and subconsciously sabotaging our businesses, lives, and freedoms because of inherited educational beliefs about intelligence and success. We both knew we had deep powers within but required a little help in breaking those chains and rising like the super stars we are!

As a coach, when Kelly approached me about working together in 2018, I welcomed her into my programme instantly, because I knew that I could help her find a way to create the business that she loved, that worked for her, her neurodiversities, her clients, the surrounding community and eventually the world.

She knew what her vision was but was struggling to create it online and put all the moving pieces together. She knew I could help her destroy and uncreate all the business "rules," "boxes," "should," and "would" that we're taught to follow and that just didn't feel right to either of us. Wellness leaders are often very creative, but can struggle to stay on task, get bored with the to-do list, and manage all the tech that is expected in modern online and face to face businesses. Kelly knew there had to be a different way, and there was! I took her through my Harmony Business Academy Programme, which is a simple step by step blueprint to help wellness leaders to produce a simple and effective business they adore, which works for them, their needs, and their clients.

Using this strategy, together we created The Stretch Zone Mind Gym! Kelly, of course, was way ahead of the wellness industry and created her online zone well before the lockdowns of 2020 and 2021! Unlike many wellness business owners, her business did not die, it accelerated, she also became a best-selling author, and wrote this book all within the pandemic!

Kelly is a unique breath of fresh air, a dyslexic genius, a tell it how it is type of person, what you see is what you get, she is a great storyteller, and shines light into the world like a beacon. This book has been long awaited in our global communities; Kelly has committed to the process for over a year now, organically using a writing blueprint by the infamous Sandra Stachowicz (8 times bestselling author), whilst embracing her truth, her skills, and as always, doing it her way!

I want to leave you with a quote I love, a quote that is dear to my heart and to show all those who have let societal beliefs, imprints and judgements block their path, that it is in their power to release those…and do it your unique, genius way!

"Emancipate yourselves from mental slavery, none but ourselves can free our minds!"

Bonus Gift

A big appreciation for reading this far.

Bonus Gift

Yoga Practice for those who like a written format

Personal Chakra Practice By Kelly Chester

<u>Props</u>

Bolster

Blocks

Blanket

Eye mask

yoga strap

Candles and incense optional

Soft music optional

2/3 mins Intention Setting

Sit on a bolster

Place two blocks on either side of the knees.

Make sure your knees are no higher than your hips.

Sit up nice and tall with a belly up and in.

Shoulders relaxed and down.

Close your eyes.

Part your lips slightly and rest your tongue behind your teeth.

Tune into your body and ensure you are comfortable.

Think about your intention.

Connect to the breath and imagine your roots are going from your Root Chakra and out through your feet and into the earth keeping you grounded and connected throughout the practice.

Now you are safe and grounded, allow yourself to feel calm and relaxed and open at the same time. Offer this practice to past hurts and relationships.

We are setting the intention on past romantic relationships and opening to the possibility of beautiful connections. We will be using a few asanas that will open the hips and the Sacral Chakra.

Place your right hand on your heart and your left hand on your lower belly and say Om three times.

Feel the vibration of the sounds.

Then say Vam three times. This universal sound connects directly to the Sacral Chakra.

Notice and feelings that may come up throughout this practice.

Go through the feeling with no expectation of the outcome. Ride through the wave of emotions that come up

And connect to the breath.

Open your eyes with a soft gaze and come back around.

2 to 3 minute Warm-up

Still sitting on the bolster. Keep your sitting bones strongly connected to the bolster. Gently fold forward, in a gentle way. Letting your body and your spine open one vertebra at a time.

Come back up and sit up nice and tall and shoulders relaxed and down.

Turn to the right side and go into a gentle twist.

Turn your head towards your right shoulder with a soft gaze with your belly lifted in and up and your Root Chakra/tailbone in the direction of the earth. Come back to the centre and repeat on the left side. Connecting to the breath and feeling the gentleness of the postures.

Come off the bolster and come onto all fours.

Child posture

From kneeling, bring big toes together and knees apart.

Sit down on heels

Rest forehead on the ground.

Reach your arms out in front of the body and turn your palms up to face the ceiling. Offer this posture to your intention to open yourself up to a loving relationship with yourself and others.

Beginners may need a blanket under the bottom and if they feel dizzy, have the chin on the floor or brick until they get used to the posture.

Option. As this is a gentle passive practice you can have your torso over a bolster and turn your head to either side for a few minutes. Such a lovely nurturing posture for a frazzled mind.

5 to 10 minute simple Asana practice

Downward dog

Step forward to tadasana

Do the rock of the pelvis back and forward, and imagine a water bucket. Water splashes back and forward over the bucket and the water gets calmer and still.

Crescent lunge pose

Plank pose into chaturanga

Upward facing dog

Downward dog

Right foot to the front into crescent lunge

Heart open chest lifting

repeat

repeat

Arms up and overhead, being mindful of the bowl of water and focusing on the passion and the breath.

Peak pose

Half splits pose

You can place a block under the thigh, or you can keep going. Breath is steady and breath into the lower belly.

Change to the other side and repeat.

Pigeon pose repeats on either side.

2 to 3 minute Cool-down Restorative

Bring your back leg around to the front and get ready to come into goddess posture

Have two blocks, a blanket, and an eye bag close by.

Place the strap behind you and let it connect to your Root Chakra. Bring your heels and toes together and tie the belt around. Let the strap connect with the inner thighs for a feeling of security. Lift from your lower belly and your chest and lie down on your bolster. Place the blocks at either side of your knees for comfort and then place the eye bag on.

If someone can help you with the blanket, then this is lovely and nurturing.

Stay here for 3 to 5 minutes for the true benefit of the posture. Opening and releasing any past hurts and emotions from your hips.

Slowly come out of the posture and take off the strap.

5 to 10 minute personal practice

Sitting up on the bolster

Repeat all the setups from the first section of the practice.

Close your eyes and imagine yourself as the best version of yourself. This practice is about opening yourself to love and that means loving yourself first and visualising how you want to be. Happy, healthy, open, and loving.

Place your hand on your heart and one onto your lower belly. I go into a cutting ties exercise using Reiki and go and meet in my mind's eye my exes or any people I feel are holding me back.

Calling in my guides and helping me safely connect and release the negative cords. I thank those that have come into my life and thank them for the lessons and gifts. I sit in the quiet and just listen and reflect. I always feel lighter after this practice.

5 mins Savasana

Either flat on your back or a bolster. Amazingly simple connection to the breath. Eye bag and blanket on and soft music.

I like the simple relaxing of each part of the body from the head down to the toes.

Simple is my favourite as we live in a terribly busy world.

I picked this personal practice because I have cleared most of my blocks and I find that lots of the hip opening and using the bolsters in restorative yoga opens the hips and works beautifully with the Reiki energy.

Healing Meditation. The Head is a Shed.

I hear this a lot, so I have created a mind clutter clearing guided meditation.

This mediation is about 11 minutes so can be done when you are short of time.

Make sure you are not driving, and you will not be disturbed.

Lay down or sit down and get pillows and blankets. Make sure you are comfortable. Now let us begin.

Relax all your muscles first starting from your forehead and then going through each of your body parts until you get all the way down to your feel.

Take a few simple breaths from your lower belly breathing in through your nose and out through your mouth. Then natural breaths throughout.

Imagine roots coming out of your feelings and grounding you into the earth. This is helping you to stay rooted and present.

Take a few more deep healing breaths.

Imagine you have a very cluttered shed. This shed represents your mind. Your mind is full of memories that no longer serve you.

You can use your imagination on this one and physically empty the shed and place the items into three piles. Ones to keep, ones to give away and ones to totally let go and throw away.

You also have a box of wires that are all tangled up. They are in a mess and can lead to overload and overwhelm. Leading to burnout, just the same as if you had too many wires connected to one socket. As you organise the wires, imagine that the knots within your body are untangling and that you are releasing tension and stress. Your body and mind are beginning to untangle and unwind. You are beginning to feel free with clear roads to aid intention setting.

You have a bonfire for things that no longer serve you, clutter clearing your physical stuff will help to clear your internal motherboard. This can include clearing social media content and followers, electronic devices and making life as simple and as clear as possible. As you clear the clutter you clear the limiting beliefs that no longer serve you. You can write these on an imaginary piece of paper. You have a fire pit near you and throw them all into the fire and let them all burn.

Allow yourself to go deeper into the relaxation. It gets darker and the sun goes down. You are engulfed in the moon's energy that is helping you to regenerate, rejuvenate and recharge. Rebooting the internal motherboard. Switching off and going into screensaver mode. The brain and the body are repairing as you rest. If your mind is in overload, then you do not go into full rest and repair so the more you do this the more you will feel the benefits of regular brain reboots. The gym for the mind will benefit the gym for your body.

Now you are in screensaver mode you can now imagine you have lots of compartments in the brain. You can organise your thoughts into files and folders, and you will wake up feeling clear and organised.

Clutter is now cleared and time to get highly creative. Your shed is empty and your wires are tidy and untangled. You have a clear space to fill up with beautiful things. You may decide to have this space completely empty, or you may fill it up with things that truly spark your joy. For example, you may have a fantastic bed that is surrounded by your favourite things. You have the most amazing sound system with all your favourite tunes that send you to another world. Whatever you design, this is your place for you to visit in your mind whenever you need to escape and take back control of your life when things become too overwhelming and too much.

Simple breathing and meditation techniques can help you to maintain balance, harmony and homeostasis reducing pain, anxiety, and many other conditions. So, when things are too bright and a bit too much. Stop and just be.

If you like the sound of this.

This is an insight into The Stretch Zone that was created by Kelly in November 2020.

Visit www.thestretchzonemindgym.co.uk to see the sessions on all the different learning formats. Audio, visual, sensory, and written.

Namaste Kelly

Acknowledgments

It has taken a village to get this book to the end result. Writing the book was the easy part even with Dyslexia. Pulling it all together took a whole community. I am not able to add everyone who has helped me to create this book and the lovely characters I have met over the years. These people gave my life meaning.

I want to thank my Grandad who always believed in me and admired how I cared for my Nanna who had Rheumatoid Arthritis from a very young age.

My mum who worked hard as a single mum to give me the freedom to live my life independently. She helped me to create a strong independent spirit.

My Aunty Janet for helping me to keep the fridge full at lean times to keep my child fed and happy.

My two best mates, Karen and Marie, for being there at every life stage and keeping me grounded and down to earth.

Jane Scanlan for helping me to create my vision in a tangible form so that people who are neurotypical can read and understand my business.

Sandra Stachowicz book strategist for bringing out my writing style whilst still keeping it in my true voice.

Mira Warszawski who has been one of my lovely friends and clients in The Stretch Zone. She is always on hand to give honest advice and feedback.

Kathryn Cartwright for editing my book and keeping it in my voice and writing style and helping it to flow so that the average reader can read it. Having dyslexia is a real challenge when keeping with the flow of writing as I have many tabs open at once.

Nicole Cartwright for bringing my vision for the cover alive. This part was hard as everyone had a different view on how they wanted my cover. I was going to have a different cover but in the end it was decided that it would be myself on the cover. No more hiding behind the mask.

My time to finally shine.

Finally, my son, Benjamin, for bringing joy and learning to my life. He has a high definition brain like me and is very gifted. He is the reason that I am writing this book to show that with the right information and environment anything is possible.

Dare to Dream.

About Kelly

Kelly is tenacious, she has boundless energy and an unstoppable watch me approach. She never gives up and is a born leader, relatable and down to earth. Kelly is a single mum and an entrepreneur.

What makes Kelly's courses unique is her ability to enable you to connect with your mind, body, and spirit using the gift of her imagination. She connects in with the energy and adapts her classes to you.

Kelly is an innovator with the way she teaches Pilates, Reiki, and Yoga using unique ways that connect with you as a client and she really gets to know what you want even before you know you want it yourself.

The ultimate benefits are more energy, standing better with ease and grace, and feeling so much more confident and in balance. Single parents, carers, or people with chronic pain are often juggling too many balls at once, so finding effortless ways to unwind rather than reach for the wine is always a plus.

Kelly is not judgmental at all and puts you at ease every step of the way and will give you that kick up the gluteal when you really need it. Her no-nonsense approach will keep you on track even on the days you do not feel like it.

Kelly is a best-selling international co-Author of Wild Women Rising, which led to her being a speaker on the BBC and other platforms talking about living with Neurodiversity and inspiring others who have hidden gifts and talents. Her Chapter on The Trials and Tribulations of a Dyslexic Genius has inspired many and led to her being a guest expert speaker for The Dyslexia Association. Kelly still maintains this relatable down to earth approach that will truly make you feel that you are in very safe hands whilst getting the results that you didn't even know yourself that you needed to address. She gets to the root. She gives you what you need and not always what you thought you wanted.

Tiny steps lead to massive rewards.

ALSO BY

Wild Women Rising - Chapter entitled, "The Trials and Tribulations of a Dyslexic Genius"

- a number #1 Amazon International Best-seller in 44 categories

Printed in Great Britain
by Amazon